# *Tricks*
## *in the*
## *City*

# Tricks in the City

## For Daring Dogs and the Humans That Love Them

### Sassafras Lowrey

TURNER
PUBLISHING COMPANY

Turner Publishing Company
Nashville, Tennessee
www.turnerpublishing.com

Cover & Layout Design: Jermaine Lau

Library of Congress Cataloging
ISBN: (p) 978-1-64250-039-4 (e) 978-1-64250-040-0
LCCN: 2019941760

BISAC category code: PET004020—PETS / Dogs / Training

Printed in the United States of America

*For my trick dogs.*

# Table of Contents

# Foreword

When you bring a dog into your household, he or she becomes part of your family. By making the effort to work with your dog on his or her first tricks, you're taking a strong step toward developing a closer bond with your dog.

With *Tricks in the City*, you will use positive training methods to build a joyful relationship with your dog, where he is a willing partner in the training process. Trick training builds relationships by deepening communication pathways, trust, and mutual respect. It offers a way to bond with your dog as you strive toward common goals and delight in your successes. The trust and cooperative spirit developed through this process will last a lifetime.

Measure your dog's success not only by the tricks they have learned, but also by improved attention and focus. Not all dogs will learn at the same rate, but your dog's success need only be measured in your eyes. While it's motivating to have a goal of a finished trick, the best thing that comes out of training your dog is the bond that develops through working together. Don't be so focused on the goal that you miss the joys of the journey!

KYRA SUNDANCE

Author of *New York Times* bestseller *101 Dog Tricks*

# From Street Dog to Champion

Charlotte has gone from a street dog to a Champion Trick Dog.

Dogs have always been an important part of my life. Even as a young child, I was fascinated with them. Everything about dogs was exciting to me: the diversity of breeds and the things that dogs were capable of learning and accomplishing alongside people. I've been infatuated with dogs for as long as I can remember, and I am at my happiest when I am spending time with dogs. To me, there is nothing more beautiful than seeing a dog and handler working together, whether herding sheep, assisting a person with disabilities, sniffing out lost people, or doing tricks. Yes, tricks! When I was a teenager, I took my passion for dog training to a new level and began training and competing in dog sports. My interest in dog sports was, at its root, about finding ways to communicate with dogs. Dog agility became my life, and I spent every weekend at dog shows and many nights a week practicing with my dogs. It wasn't until adulthood that I got involved with tricks and trick training but, once I did, I've never looked back.

I first got involved in tricks with my dog Charlotte. Charlotte is a former street dog. She was found living on the streets of a small Southern town where she'd had a litter of puppies. She managed to keep her puppies alive on the streets until they were captured and brought to an overcrowded shelter. Charlotte was severely malnourished and about half of what her healthy body weight should be. Right before she was to be euthanized, a rescue pulled Charlotte (and her puppies) out and transported them north to NYC, where my partner and I were living at the time. I met Charlotte walking down the street en route to the grocery store. She was peering out the window of an adoption van, and I had what I would consider an actual spiritual experience. I knew that dog in the window was my dog, and in that moment, I knew my life would never be the same.

Charlotte is not what anyone would consider an easy dog. She's an incredibly smart dog, but Charlotte also has a host of behavioral and anxiety issues resulting from her traumatic start in life. She is extremely reactive to dogs she doesn't know, and has severe clinical anxiety and phobias to changes in barometric pressure, thunder storms, and fireworks. Charlotte is, shall we say, not a dog for everyone, but she was the perfect dog for me. Since bringing her home, my number-one goal for Charlotte has been to give her the biggest world possible. In an effort to reach Charlotte, I spent a lot of time working on building a world that was safe and full and fun for her. This ultimately led my partner and me to sell our inner Brooklyn apartment and purchase a house for her, first in outer Brooklyn, where she could have a yard, and then later relocating across the country to Portland, Oregon, in large part to be in a part of the country with fewer environmental triggers, as her anxiety/panic conditions were resistant to medication management. Charlotte is the most sensitive dog I have ever shared my life with, and she's also probably the smartest dog I have ever worked with. Despite all her behavioral challenges, tricks became something that Charlotte would look forward to working on daily. Through trick training, she was certainly not cured—lifelong management and ongoing work around her issues is a daily reality for us—but the training became something we could incorporate into stressful situations to defuse them for her. The more tricks I taught Charlotte, the more I began to understand what a profound difference tricks were making in her life, and our life together. I started to explore more about tricks and discovered competitive tricks, a sport where you are able to compete remotely from anywhere by submitting tricks for titles via video.

This was perfect for a dog like Charlotte, who would be way over threshold and uncomfortable in a traditional dog show/trial environment. The structure of trick titles gave me a training goal to work toward and a strategy for structuring our daily training schedule. Swiftly, Charlotte began accumulating titles, and I was hooked. Over the years, I wanted to take my commitment to tricks to a new level and became officially part of the organization Do More With Your Dog, the first trick dog titling organization. I also became a Certified Trick Dog Instructor (CTDI), meaning I have been certified to approve trick dogs for titles since 2013, and I support others getting involved in the sport. Since that time, I have earned bronze, silver, and gold trainer level distinctions in recognition of the number of titles that I have observed for dogs all over the world, and in 2018 I earned the Trainer of the Year special distinction. Along the way, I kept up with trick training my own dogs. I was so proud the day that Charlotte earned her Champion Trick Dog Title (the highest title that a trick dog can receive)! It was nothing short of remarkable to think that, just a few short years before, she had been a discarded dog that no one cared about, living on the streets, and she now had a loving family and a fulfilled life, and was even a champion! I'm continually in awe of her resilience and her ability to play and find joy. I consider myself so lucky that I get to share my life with her, and the world of trick sports she has opened up for me.

I now have three dogs, and trick training is a huge part of our life together. My youngest, Sirius, began learning tricks the day she came home, flying through trick titles, earning her Champion Trick Dog Title right after her second birthday, and becoming only the second Newfoundland dog in the world to earn the highest trick dog title. I'm passionate about tricks, not only because they are a lot of fun, but even more so because of the capacity for trick training to really bring people and their dogs together in new ways.

Regardless of whether you have any interest in competing, trick training is something that every dog and guardian can get involved with. As we will discuss, trick training can and will strengthen the relationship you have with your dog.

Happy Trick Training!

Sassafras
February 2019

Art by Nicole J. Georges of Sassafras and her trick dogs.

Chapter 1

# Why Tricks & How Dogs Learn

Trick training is a great way to have fun with your dogs.

Photo credit: Kathleen Tepperies

Welcome to *Tricks in the City*! If you're here, you probably have the best dog in the world and you're looking for ways to have more fun with your pup, and maybe even teach them an impressive trick or two. Trick training is something that all dogs (and people) can have fun with together, and the best thing is, you don't need any kind of expensive equipment, and you don't have to travel anywhere to do it. Trick training can happen in your living room or on your daily walks. All you need is a little bit of time, and some treats!

I used to think that this training was just something fun to do with dogs, and it absolutely is, but I've also seen firsthand the way that trick training can literally transform a dog's life. It also has the capacity to foster a stronger relationship between people and their dogs. Trick training can take you and your dogs in many directions—not only is it fun, it is also the foundation for the work that animal actors are doing when we see them in our favorite movies and on TV. Trick training is a tremendous amount of fun, and it's something that everyone (even kids) can do with any dog, from the youngest puppy to the oldest senior pooch. Dogs are hardwired to want to work with us and please us, and I'm no biologist, but I believe that we're pretty hardwired to want to work with dogs; we just don't always know how to communicate with one another. If you are looking to find ways to spend more time with your dog, or if you and your dog already spend a lot of time training but you're looking for something low-pressure to enjoy together, trick training is perfect for you!

Training should always be fun for you and, most importantly, for your dog. Dogs learn best when they are getting "paid," so as we start to teach tricks, we are going to be using lots of treats and/or toys. Basically, whatever is most motivating to your dogs is what we are going to be using. As trick trainers, our goal is to make instructions to our dogs as clear as possible, and make training as fun as possible. Any kind of training that resorts to pain, intimidation, or fear (such as "alpha dynamics") is not only cruel and inhumane, but has been scientifically proven to be ineffective and damaging to the relationship between dog and guardian. The same is true for prong collars and shock collars (or e-collars, as they are becoming commonly referred to).

Training your dog and spending time with your dog should be fun. We don't want to do anything that will in any way hurt your relationship with one another, which is what pain-based or punitive training does.

# Why Tricks?

Ann Cress' Boerboel Tsavo loves learning and showing off!

Who doesn't love seeing a dog do a cute trick? It brings a smile to our faces, it's fun and stimulating for dogs, so it's no wonder that trick training is one of the fastest-growing canine sports. Not only have tricks become a competitive dog sport, they have always been and remain an excellent way to bond with the dog you share your home and life with. Dogs love learning and they love spending quality time with us, where we put down our phones, stop watching movies, and turn all of our attention to them. Tricks are perfect for this. In just a few minutes of practice together every day, not only will you be positively investing in your relationship with your best friend, but your dog will also be on her way to learning an array of tricks.

Unlike a lot of other dog sports that require complicated, big, and usually expensive equipment, trick training is something you can do in the comfort of your own home. You don't need to go out and find a professional trainer or sign up for classes; you can teach your dog tricks in your living room, in your backyard, and on your daily walks. But tricks go beyond just something fun to do with your dog (though they are certainly that too)—trick training can literally change your dog's life. Learning tricks is confidence-boosting, especially for nervous, shy, or anxious dogs. Trick training can be extremely helpful for dogs who are reactive or struggling with anxiety, to help them to learn more about learning, and to gain confidence in new situations. That said, none of the trick training advice in this book can or should take the place of working directly with a positive-reinforcement-based trainer or animal behaviorist who is skilled and experienced with dogs who have reactivity, panic, or other anxiety-related behavioral conditions.

Trick training is so versatile, it can be done anytime anywhere, and you can gradually incorporate tricks your dog loves and is confident with into situations where they might be less sure of themself or their surroundings. I used to see trick training as something fun to do on occasion with my dogs, but I've come to understand it to be essential for supporting them in navigating our busy urban worlds. I now consider trick training to be a core part of socializing any puppy, or new adult dog entering my family—it's that important! One of my favorite things about trick training is how mentally and physically good it is for dogs. Trick training is extremely mentally stimulating, which makes it a perfect activity to enjoy with your dogs if you live in an apartment and don't have a big yard (and even if you do). Working with your dog can be significantly more enriching than a long off-leash run! I'm not kidding! If the weather is crummy and you don't want to take your dog on a long walk, pull out some treats and start teaching tricks. You might be surprised at how mentally well-exercised your dog is at the end of the training session, and how that can lead to a dog who is much more likely to be ready to curl up on the couch and watch a movie with you at the end of the day. On the physical side of things, trick training can also promote great muscle tone and strength training for dogs of all ages. There are, of course, safety concerns, and you want to make sure that any tricks you are teaching your dogs aren't going to be too physically demanding for them. In this book, I have primarily focused on low-impact tricks, and I have tried to highlight the tricks that are the highest impact and flag them as likely not appropriate for very young and very old dogs, as well as any dog who has any kind of ongoing health or orthopedic conditions. In general, if you ever have questions or concerns about the safety or appropriateness of a trick for your dog, contact your veterinarian before training.

## Tricks for All

There is a very common old myth and figure of speech that "you can't teach an old dog new tricks." Honestly, I think this is one of the most dangerous pieces of misinformation permeating modern dog culture. Not that I think all dogs need to learn how to jump through hoops or find hidden odors in order to live a happy life (though it does bring a lot of joy to many dogs)—rather, what concerns me is the underlying idea that older dogs are incapable of learning. This is really sad for these dogs. Old dogs are fantastic and smart, and they absolutely need to be trained and enriched the same way younger dogs do.

My oldest dog, Mercury, is sixteen and a half years old (at the time of this writing) and only ten pounds. He's my retired service dog, so he absolutely has had a lot of training in his life, and has been defying expectations about what small dogs can and can't do since he was a little puppy. Now he leads a quiet life of retirement, but that doesn't mean he doesn't have enrichment. Even as his health has gone up and down—he has in the last year lost some of his vision—that doesn't mean he has stopped trick training. Any time I pull out my treat pouch, he's ready to go and eager to keep up with his much younger, much bigger sisters. I believe that trick training is a big part of why he has done so well over the years and adjusted so seamlessly to loss of sight. His brain is always active and learning new things. I believe this is part of what has kept him so active and healthy even at his advanced age.

All dogs can learn tricks.
Photo credit: Veronica Tan

## All Shapes and Sizes

Unfortunately, another stereotype that persists around trick training is that it's only for large dogs, or breeds that are traditionally considered to be "athletic" or "smart," like border collies. This couldn't be further from the truth. Every single dog is capable of learning and having fun with trick training. Not only can dogs never be too old to learn new tricks, trick training is something that dogs of all sizes, breeds, and builds can have fun participating in. Small dogs can be excellent trick dogs just as larger dogs can. People mistakenly think that tricks are only for large dogs, but they really aren't! While some dogs are physically more suited to certain tricks—for example, I don't want my hundred-pound puppy learning to jump into my arms—there are tricks that are safe and fun for all dogs.

At the end of the day, trick training is about building your relationship with your dog. The relationship that you and your dog have with one another is something that is continually evolving and growing. The more quality time you spend together, actually engaging with your dog, the stronger a relationship you will have. It breaks my heart when I hear people say that their dog is dumb, or incapable of learning. Your dog is brilliant—they're just waiting for you to help them understand what you want, and training is the way to go about that. Trick training won't solve behavior problems you might be having, but it will strengthen the relationship you have with your dog and cut down on nuisance behaviors your dog might be getting into out of boredom or being under-stimulated.

Trick training isn't just parlor tricks. Trick training is about relationship building and confidence-boosting, not only for our dogs, but for us as well! Sometimes it can feel overwhelming or discouraging to be responsible for the welfare, education, and care of a dog. I hear this a lot, especially from people deep in the throes of puppy socialization, or from individuals who have rescued an adult dog who may have had a traumatic start in life and is coming with some baggage. Working with your dog can feel discouraging as you work through behavioral challenges or develop appropriate management strategies to keep your dog and others safe. It can be easy to miss the little ways that you are building a stronger bond with your dog or making small, incremental growth in training. Tricks can be a quick and easy way to build your dog's confidence and your confidence as a teacher, and, most importantly, to have fun together.

All day every day, we are teaching our dogs; we're educating them about what we want in terms of behavior in any given situation. It's a huge responsibility, it can feel overwhelming, but it can also be a lot of fun. I've never met a dog who isn't capable of enthusiastically learning. Tricks (including competitive trick titling) are accessible to differently abled dogs, including dogs who are deaf, blind, or have mobility issues. Because of the diversity of tricks that you can teach your dog, there are tricks that will fit the specialized needs and limitations of any dog.

Chapter 2

# Getting Started

Are you sold? Let's get started training tricks! To get started, you need to figure out how your dog wants to be paid. Yes, you have to pay the dog! Put your wallet away—money might be motivating to you, but it won't likely be very motivating for your dog (not to mention that coins are a choking hazard). For teaching tricks, you'll be paying your dog in currency that is valuable to dogs: food and toys.

## What You Need

Treats—when you work, you want to get paid. So does your dog! Treat training is really important. I sometimes hear people say that they don't want to train with treats because they want their dog to work for the sure joy of working with them...do you work just because you get satisfaction from working? Probably not. Your dog is the same way—they want to get paid for their work and they deserve to be paid. Yes, our dogs love us, but we need to keep building that relationship and "paying" or rewarding our dogs for a job well done.

As you start getting ready to begin trick training, your first task will be to find out what different levels of reward look like to your dog. For many dogs, the smellier, softer treats are going to have the highest value. Either commercially manufactured treats or things like hot dogs and string cheese are the favorites of most of my dogs, but each dog is different. My youngest dog is most excited by dry biscuits (why, no one knows!). What matters most is that your dog thinks what you are offering is high-value, so try out different treats and note what gets your dog the most excited.

Sometimes finding your dog's currency requires a little bit of trial and error. It also might require you to do some carrying of treats—what is high-value today might be less high-value tomorrow, so you'll have to pull out something else. I like to rotate the treats I'm giving when training among different high-value ones. Find your dog's currency—even if it isn't high-value to you, it might be to them! Different dogs will find different things valuable. Try different treats and play to see what motivates your dog most and use that. As you are finding your dog's currency, also experiment with play and toys. You'll still need to have high-value treats for some training, but for some tricks, if your dog is toy-motivated, start to incorporate different toys. A lot of working dogs, like search and rescue, police, and military dogs, work for play and toys (retrieve, and especially tug), so if your dog is most excited about toys, they are in good company.

Even if toys are the highest-value reward to your dog, you will want to have a variety of treats available when you're training—you can even incorporate your dog's kibble into your training! Just reserve kibble or other lower-value treats for practicing trick skills that your dog is already confident and having fun with, and pull out the higher-value treats when you are teaching something new, or practicing in a new or more distracting location.

## Safety First

If you are training outside and not in a fenced yard, it's important to always have your dog on leash. The best thing to have is a plain six-foot nylon or leather leash. Avoid retractable leashes, because they can cause a lot of injury to you and/or your dog and don't give you a lot of control over where your dog is. Following leash laws is a simple but important part of being a good canine citizen. Dogs aren't robots; even if you think your dog has a good recall, they likely don't—if another animal ran past and you called your dog, would he immediately turn and return to you? If yes, that's fantastic, but still keep the leash on, for the comfort and safety of other dogs and members of the community. Following leash laws, scooping poop, and keeping your dog(s) close to you and under your control helps to make the general public more accepting of us having our dogs with us in (dog-friendly) places, and keeps places dog-friendly and welcoming to all of our dogs. You'll also want to have your dog on a collar, head halter, or chest harness. Safe options include flat collars (nylon or leather), limited-slip martingales (which tighten down to a point that keeps a dog from backing out of a collar, but don't constrict the dog's breathing), head halters (like the halters horses wear), and back or front clip harnesses are all safe options for your dog if you are walking or trick training in public spaces. Be sure to avoid prong collars, choke chains, and shock collars/ e-collars—pain conditioning should have no place in dog training.

## Teaching Your Dog about Learning

Dogs are not born knowing how to communicate with us—or rather, they aren't born knowing what our words mean. Over time, your dog learns about how to interact with you; they learn what our likes and dislikes are, what our words and gestures and body language mean. Our dogs are always learning from us, every moment of every day. Our dogs learn good things that we want, like to go potty outside, but our dogs are also learning not-so-good things, like that they don't have to come until you say "come," "cooooooooommmmmeeeeeee," "plleeeeaaaaassssseee coooommmmmeeeee," ten times and jump up and down. When we don't set our dogs up for success, when we aren't clear about our expectations for them and don't create circumstances where they are going to be successful, we often end up training our dogs in things we don't mean to (for example, that "come" isn't a verbal cue in and of itself, and that when we want our dogs to come, we will do that whole literal dance and say "come" a bunch of times). This doesn't mean that you need to "teach your dog who is boss" or otherwise force them. Quite the opposite, our goal with training should be to make working with us the most fun option, eliminating the opportunity for our dogs to make mistakes—so, for example, only taking your dog into your yard or to the park on leash with lots of high-value treats, so you can support and reward the "come" recall to the point when the behavior is solidly understood by your dog and they think it's a lot of fun to come racing back because it doesn't mean the end to play, it means yummy treats and more playing. We want to make engaging with us the most rewarding option available to our dogs.

Next to treats, patience is the most important thing to have when you are starting to teach your dog tricks. We talk to our dogs all day long, but a lot of what we say doesn't make sense to them. Dogs don't come pre-programmed to understand what different words mean. Training your dog is about building a relationship and developing a shared language. Your dog has to learn what those random noises coming out of your mouth mean, and the only way that can happen is with positive training, patience, and fun repetition. Our dogs are going to get confused or make mistakes, but nothing they are doing is really a mistake. If our dog fails to do a trick in the way we want them to, it means that they aren't ready for the level of difficulty. It's a moment for us to step back and help our dogs to be successful.

## No Punishment

There is no place for punishment in tricks. If you find yourself getting overwhelmed and frustrated, it's time to give your dog a treat and take a break. There are a lot of reasons not to punish your dog in general—causing your dog pain or fear or discomfort while learning is contradictory to the learning you want your dog to do, and doesn't help them to retain information. Ideas like your dog needing to be dominated or shown who is "alpha" have been discredited by canine behavior and training researchers. Dogs are not "mini wolves"; they are not looking at us as "pack leaders." Essentially, you want training with your dog to come from a place of mutual respect and fun. All training, especially trick training, should be enjoyable for both of you, not something that makes your dog overwhelmed or shut down.

## Positive Reinforcement

I define positive-reinforcement-based training as methods that come from a place of mutual respect, without use of fear, pain, or intimidation. Basically, this means training that centers the relationship between the person and the animal, and doesn't use tools like shock collars/e-collars and prong collars that cause pain to communicate what the human wants.

## Clicker Training

One method of positive reinforcement training that is useful for all animals, from puppies to goldfish, is clicker training. Clicker training is based on marking a desired behavior and then providing a reward for it. The reason that a clicker (those little box-shaped devices that are sold for about a dollar on the counter of most pet shops, that have a button and make a metallic "click" noise when pressed) works is because trainers are able to deliver the click more clearly, quickly, and more precisely than a verbal marker or food reward alone. The approach grew out of trainers working with marine mammals, and has taken the dog training industry by storm because of its ease and effectiveness. Basically, clicker training lets us communicate more clearly with all animals, from cats and horses and rats to wildlife like dolphins and zebras! Yes, really— the same methods people use to teach an elephant, you can use to teach your dog! Pretty cool, right?

Clicker training is successful because it allows trainers to clearly "mark" (a.k.a. communicate to the dog) that they have performed a specific behavior that is desirable, and then come in and reward with a treat. Essentially, it allows us to improve our communication with our dogs as we are training, because the clicker is such a clear signal to our dogs (once they're properly introduced to it) that we can use it to mark very small behavior cues, enabling us to train very impressive and specific tricks, like dunking a ball in a basketball hoop.

If you want to give clicker training a go, get a clicker (again you can find them inexpensively at most pet stores) and a bowl of very small pieces of very high-value treat. When you first introduce clicker training to your dog, your only goal is for your dog to associate the click with something great (the treat). So, you will click, and treat, click and treat, several times in a row. At this stage, we aren't asking for any kind of behaviors from the dog—we just want them to start making the connection that the click means good things (treats) are coming.

After a couple of short training sessions like that, ask your dog to do something they already know how to do, like "sit," and, right as they get into the

Sirius and I had a wonderful time at Clicker Expo 2019.

appropriate position, click, praise, and treat. Repeat a few times. The goal is for our dogs to understand that the click is our way of telling them that what they are doing in that moment is what we want when we give them a specific cue.

Keep your training sessions short when introducing the clicker and all the other training we are going to be doing. A few short (five minutes or less) training sessions spread through the day is much more effective (and fun) for your dog than one long training session. My goal with training is to always end a session with my dog having been successful and having had fun—essentially, you want to end with your dog wanting to do more, not bored and frustrated.

If you are interested in learning more about clicker training, check out the work of Karen Pryor, Karen Pryor Academy, and her Clicker Expo annual conference. Learn more at karenpryoracademy.com. If you are interested in animal behavior and training and have the opportunity to attend Clicker Expo, I can't recommend it highly enough. They also have a variety of online learning opportunities, and a growing number of positive-reinforcement-based trainers across the country and around the world are incorporating clicker training into their classes.

## Patience

Dog training can be exhausting and overwhelming. We're communicating with a completely different species, and sometimes asking them to do very unnatural things, like putting a little ball into a little basketball hoop! It's important to make sure that you train when you are in a good mood and in a good place to keep your training sessions fun and positive. Different dogs learn at different speeds. Don't compare your dog with someone else's dog, or, if you share your life with multiple dogs, don't compare one dog to another. Different dogs learn differently, and even learn different kinds of tricks at different speeds. For example, my dog Charlotte learns anything with small details very quickly, but is much slower to learn tricks that require her to position her body in certain ways, a skill set that my youngest dog, Sirius, excels at.

Our dogs are individuals; there are some tricks that your dog will enjoy more than others. Our dogs learn through repetition; again, you want to train more frequently in short, fun training sessions with lots of toys and treats. Dogs do learn through repetition, but you can do too much of a good thing. No one likes a drill sergeant (even a fun one), so, if you find your dog seeming to be a little less enthusiastic in your training sessions, you might have just worked a certain behavior a little too much for the moment. It's important to keep your training sessions varied and short. Work on teaching a new trick alongside practicing a trick your dog has successfully mastered, and always be sure to end each training session on a positive note—create an opportunity for your dog to be successful, even if that means having to lower the criteria of what you are asking for. Keep your training sessions short and sweet. A few short (under-five-minute) training sessions a few times a day will be more effective than one forty-five-minute training session.

HINT: If your dog isn't consistently successful in your training sessions, it's probably because you are asking for too much too soon. Slow down, make the criteria easier, and then slowly build up to the full behavior that you are trying to achieve.

# Ways of Training

There are a variety of techniques we will be utilizing to support your dog in understanding the tricks we want to teach them. When our dogs are first learning a trick or skill, this is how we will show them what we want them to do, or communicate to them what we want them to do.

## Luring

This is pretty much what it sounds like: we will be using treats to lure or maneuver our dog into the desired position. Luring is a fast and easy way to teach a lot of tricks, because we are able to use treats to lead them to a behavior or position that we want. So, for example, your dog's nose follows the treat, the body follows, and your dog ends up in the position you want—say "sit," for example. You click and/or praise and give your dog the treat. As your dog gets more comfortable with the behavior, you are able to phase out the physical lure.

## Shaping

With shaping, your dog is actually getting to put together the pieces of the trick without your prompting or leading. Shaping easily goes hand in hand with clicker training (though you can also use a verbal marker). With shaping, you are clicking or marking very small incremental behavioral changes while engaging with an object. The exciting thing about shaping as a training methodology is that your dog is actively thinking and puzzling out the behavior, which can be very rewarding, empowering, and confidence-building for them, creating a training conversation between you and your dog. An example of what this would look like is: if you wanted to teach your dog to push a ball with their nose, you might take out a beach ball and have a clicker (or be ready with a verbal marker your dog is familiar with, like "yes") and a lot of treats. To start, you will click and treat for any movement toward the ball, then click and treat for sniffing at the ball. If your dog paws at the ball, you would just ignore that, and then when the dog sniffs the ball hard enough to push it, you would click, praise, and jackpot, giving lots of treats. Your dog is essentially puzzling out what kind of engagement with the ball gets the reward, and will offer more of the behaviors that are getting rewarded, thus creating the finished trick, to which you can then add a verbal cue.

## Capturing

This isn't always the fastest way to teach a trick, but it is a really fun process, and can be extremely effective for teaching tricks that are physically subtle (like head tilts, shaking, licking, leg lifting, etc.). To teach a trick via capturing, you will be clicking and/or verbally marking something your dog does, each time you see them do it. So, for example, if you want to teach your dog to shake on cue, each time you see them shake off after waking up or coming in from the rain, you will click, praise, and treat, and begin adding in a verbal marker, like "shake." With time and repetition, your dog will begin to figure out that they are being rewarded for shaking their body and that the verbal marker you have attached to it—"shake" in this example—will become your cue to ask your dog to perform the behavior at any time.

## Signals

As we get into the trick training, we will be using both verbal and physical cues or signals to our dogs to indicate what trick we want them to be doing. These signals are the way our dogs know what tricks we want them to do. Here's an overview of how we will be communicating with our dogs as we teach them tricks.

1. Just like it sounds, a **verbal signal** is a word that we have taught our dogs to associate with a specific trick or physical behavior we want them to do.

2. With **physical signals,** which are often, though not always, hand signals, your dog associates the physical cue with the trick you want them to do. Dogs are extremely attuned to our body language, and so are very responsive to physical cues, alone or paired with verbal signals. Dogs are consistently watching our bodies, so they often take very quickly to physical cues. For tricks taught via luring, the physical cue can often be a less exaggerated form of the way you initially lured the behavior, something your dog will already be familiar with at that point.

## Building Duration

With some tricks, we want our dog to perform the behavior and keep moving by, say, weaving between our legs while we walk—we don't want them to stop because we would then probably trip over them and fall! Not fun! With other tricks, like "sit," you might want your dog to stay in position until you tell them to do something else or release them. It's very easy to build duration in your tricks by continuing to reward behavior in position (by treating while they stay), and then, when your dog is familiar with the behavior, upping the criteria before you reward. This means increasing the amount of time between your dog getting into position and your click/reward, and then adding in a release word.

A release word or cue is something that communicates to your dog that a stationary behavior has finished and they can move. An example of this would be a verbal cue to release your dog from a sit or a down they have been holding. You can use this release word in trick training and in everyday life (trick training is of course part of our daily life with our dogs), so if you have asked your dog to stay, you want to clearly communicate to them when they can move. By building duration skills into our dogs' training vocabulary, we can also communicate to them our expectation that, when performing a stationary trick (like sit, down, bow, or beg), they should hold that trick until released.

To build duration, you will need to pick a word you want to use for release. I like to pick something that isn't a part of my general vocabulary, so that I don't inadvertently cue my dog to move when they are in a stay, or at another time when I don't mean to. "Okay" and "Break" are common release words. I like to do a little extra and tend to have a flair for being a bit more eccentric in my dog training, so I use words/phrases with my own dogs that are a bit unusual. I also like to have a different release word for each of my dogs, so that I can release each one individually while the other dogs hold position. This is handy when I have the dogs all doing tricks at the same time, and in real life with three dogs, when for example I want to release one dog at a time from a stay to get meals, or from their crates. I like to find words that fit my dog's personalities or somehow connect to their names. Mercury's release word is "Blast-Off," Charlotte's is "Mosey," and Sirius's is "Apparate" (yes, the Harry Potter spell). Come up with a release word that you like and then, to get your dog familiar with it, start when they are lying down on their own—take out a treat, and toss it. As your dog gets up to follow the treat, say your release word in a happy voice, praise, and let your dog get the treat. Repeat a few times. The goal is for your dog to understand that the release word is a cue to move. After a few practice sessions with throwing the treat, get your dog's attention and say the release word. When your dog gets up, toss several treats, give lots of praise, have a little party!

## Treats

Treats are one of the most important parts of the trick training we are going to do. To support the learning process, and to reward the work your dog is doing, you want to have an abundance of treats that are motivating to them.

When starting to train, a lot of people want to know when they can stop giving their dogs treats as part of trick training. My simple answer is NEVER! Do you want to work for free? But that isn't actually true. You will, as your dog gains confidence and familiarity with tricks, be able to start to phase out the need to, for example, lure your dog into the trick. You will begin asking your dog to execute a particular trick perhaps even without food in your hand. Your treats might be sitting next to you, or in a treat pouch attached to your waistband. I know, I know, not the sexiest look, but hey, I've been seeing fanny packs making a comeback in NYC and gracing fashion runways. This is great news for hip dog people like yourself. Don't be afraid to keep dog treats on you at all times. You like to get paid for a job well done; so does your dog!

Try not to be in a rush to remove treats from your training plan. A lot of people want to cut treats out as fast as possible in order to prove (mostly to themselves) that the dog really understands. Don't rush! You want to really make sure that your dog understands what is expected of them before you increase the criteria or make the game significantly harder, such as by taking away treats. I promise you won't always have to lure your dog into sitting with a piece of hotdog, but if you try to remove treats too quickly or ask too much of your dog before they really understand the game you're playing together, your end trick is going to be inconsistent and sloppy. It also will add stress and tension to your relationship with your dog. Dogs want to play with us, they want to work with us. Dogs don't want to irritate or frustrate us. Part of being an ethical play partner for our dogs is to communicate as clearly as we possibly can to them.

As your dog becomes familiar with the tricks you are teaching, you will want to begin phasing out the reward. You just won't need to pay at a one-trick, one-cookie ratio anymore. You might ask your dog to do a couple of tricks before treating. The more experienced your dog is, the more you can vary your treat delivery. Sometimes you will reward for every trick (especially if it's a more challenging trick, or a trick being performed in a new or distracting environment). Other times you'll want to only reward after a few repetitions. The key is to vary when you treat—sometimes after two repetitions, sometimes after several—so your dog is kept motivated.

Chapter 3

# Safety First!

Trick training is a lot of fun, it's great for your dog emotionally, it's fantastic for your bond with your dog, and it can even improve your dog's overall health by keeping them physically active and increasing or maintaining muscle tone. Trick training is something that any dog of any age can participate in. However, not all tricks are appropriate for all dogs. A lot of the tricks I'm going to be covering in this book are what we call low-impact, meaning they are not likely to cause any kind of stress to your dog's joints or muscles. However, there are other tricks, especially those that involve jumping, that are going to have a harder impact on your dog's body and are not appropriate for senior dogs, puppies whose joints are still developing, and dogs with medical conditions. While puppies are very active, their joints are still developing and soft; for large and very large dogs, this period of growth is longer and can extend for well over a year. During this period, a dog's growth plates are not closed, meaning their bones are soft and can be easily injured, which can impact your dog's health for life. Talk with your vet before doing any strenuous training with your dog, and with large and very large dogs, you will want to have x-rays taken to confirm that your young dog's growth plates are closed and that it is safe for your dog to begin jumping.

There are a lot of trainers offering conditioning classes in person and online. Be sure to inquire about their qualifications before signing your dog up. Conditioning and working on overall fitness is very important for all dogs, especially dogs who will be doing a lot of high-impact trick training; however, inappropriate conditioning can also cause injuries.

Online and especially on social media, there are a growing number of viral videos showing dogs doing all kinds of "impressive" stunts or tricks. As you would expect with a viral video, in most of these videos, the dogs doing the tricks are very well-trained and execute the tricks (at least in the video) without injury; however, they are very dangerous, often involving dogs being high up on platforms or walls, dogs jumping to extreme heights (even if your dog can jump quite high, that doesn't mean we ever want to ask them to do so), or dogs engaging with dangerous props like fire. When we get to jumping tricks, we will discuss this, along with what are considered safe jumping heights for your dog to work up to, but the general rule of thumb is that anything higher than your dog's head is too high to jump safely (even if they are capable of jumping higher).

Before doing any kind of high-impact trick training, or any other canine sport training including jumping, it's a good idea to talk with your dog's veterinarian to explore your dog's overall wellness levels, and whether there are any health restrictions you should keep in mind when training them or any tricks you should avoid teaching. If you have a dog with a history of orthopedic issues, it's a very good idea to talk with a physical therapist, in addition to your regular vet, before trick training. My youngest dog, Sirius, despite coming from a wonderful breeder and a breed line that had had all possible testing to ensure joint health, was diagnosed with torn cruciate ligaments in her knees before her second birthday, requiring major reconstructive surgery—even though she had never done anything high-impact in terms of trick/sport training or just in general life (for example, never jumping into or out of a car). I was thrilled to discover that, after her knees were surgically reconstructed and we began physical therapy with a certified physical therapist, many of the exercises that we were prescribed related right back to the kind of low-impact trick training my puppy had been doing since the first day she came home.

Even if your dog is in peak health, with medical clearance from your veterinarian, it's important to be thoughtful and cautious about what kinds of tricks you ask your dog to do, and on what surfaces you ask them to do them (especially high-impact jumping tricks). Avoid asking your dog to jump on concrete, hardwood floors, tile, or any other hard and/or slippery surface. Carpet, grass, and dirt are the best options for footing. Dogs trust us to keep them safe. Just because they can do something doesn't mean they should. Dogs rely on us to make good decisions for them, so don't break your dog's trust in you by putting them (or any part of their body) in harm's way to perfect a cool-looking trick, or to get a video to upload on social media.

Chapter 4

# Tricks to Teach

Though some of these tricks may seem more like basic obedience than trick training, they are no less tricky for your dog! Dogs don't come pre-programmed, knowing what pop culture has taught us are basic tricks. Our job in teaching dogs tricks involves translating our language and finding ways to communicate more clearly with our dogs, so that we can develop a shared language.

**Remember:** Keep your training sessions short and fun! Don't make this like practicing for an elementary school spelling test or drilling multiplication tables. You want your dog to have as much fun with trick training as you do. In order to do this, you want to keep your dog successful. If you find yourself getting frustrated or irritated while teaching a new trick, take a break! Never scold or punish your dog while training. Use lots of treats and lots of toys!

When teaching a new trick, it can be tempting to work it and work it and work it until you get it right. And then, once your dog is doing it, it's tempting to do it again and again, both to make sure your dog has it right, and because it's just so cute to watch them doing the trick. This is a great way to overwhelm your dog and burn them out. I like to keep my training sessions to about five minutes, several times a day. You want to stop a training session while your dog is still having fun and engaged.

# Tips

* You don't have to call these tricks what I call them. Because dogs don't come understanding human languages, you can call the tricks whatever you want. The most important thing is CONSISTENCY. Once you pick a word and/or a physical cue for a behavior, make sure you're doing the same thing each time to keep your dog from becoming confused and frustrated while you are training.

* Practice, practice, practice! As your dog becomes consistent with a trick at home, start working on the trick in your backyard, or in the hallway of your apartment building, at the park, at the vet, while you're waiting outside a café for someone to go inside and bring you out a coffee and bagel (never ever leave your dog tied outside a shop even for a moment! There is an epidemic of dognapping, and it only takes a split second for your dog to be stolen, held for ransom, sold to dogfighters, abused, rehomed, etc.—just don't do it!). Every moment you spend with your dog is a training opportunity. Dogs are situational learners, so that cool trick your dog has mastered in your living room will be a lot trickier on a busy sidewalk. Go slowly when asking for the trick in a new environment. Even if your dog doesn't need a lure at home, don't forget to bring one out when you are introducing the trick to a new space the first few times. It will help your dog make the connection to a trick they know in a new and distracting environment.

# 1
## Sit

Daisy is an expert-level trick dog and nationally certified Human Remains Detection K9 who loves her job.

Photo credit: Christa Tucker

# 1. Sit

- Take a treat and, with your dog either in front of you or at your side, place the treat right in front of their nose but don't let them have it yet (it's okay if they're nibbling or licking at it).

- Pull the treat up and slightly back toward their back. Your dog's nose should follow the treat.

- As your dog's head goes up and back, their bottom will go down.

- As soon as their bottom touches the floor, click or verbally mark with a "yes!" and give them the treat.

- Repeat this a few times. When you are confident that your dog is going to follow the treat, you can begin to use the word "sit," or whatever word you want to use to cue that behavior, right before their bottom touches the floor, and then praise and treat!

- Slowly, you can begin to lure your dog into sitting position without a treat in your hand, and then give the treat once your dog is in the position.

- This will be true with other tricks as well: timing is very important. Make sure you are giving the treat while your dog is still in position, that is, before the dog gets up. By treating in position, you are making sure that your dog understands that this behavior, the thing they are doing right now, as their favorite treat is going into their mouth, is what you want them to be doing.

# Tips

*   If your dog backs up or tries to jump up instead of sitting, it's likely that the treat is just a little too high. Try to lower the treat, keeping it right on your dog's nose, and lure them back smoothly.

*   Words have power! Don't be in a huge rush to start asking your dog to sit outside of your training sessions.

    Example: if you ask your dog to sit when they're barking because someone is at the door, and they don't yet really solidly know what "sit" means, the likelihood their butt is going to hit the floor is...almost zero. It is far more rewarding for your dog to continue to bark at the door, especially if they aren't exactly sure what the word means. Remember, dogs don't come pre-programmed to understand our language. This will be true for future tricks as well. Practice, practice, practice, in controlled settings where your dog is set up to succeed.

# 2
## Down

## 2. Down

Down is one of those tricks that, unfortunately, many people think dogs should come pre-programmed knowing how to do. And dogs do know how to do "down"—they lie down all the time—but they don't actually know what the word "down" means. Teaching down is an important trick because it is a foundation trick. By this I mean it is a behavior that is going to be incorporated into a number of other tricks that we're going to teach later on—like roll over, splat or play dead, etc.

There are a couple of ways that dogs might naturally perform the "down" behavior, so there are two ways you can teach your dog to down. Some dogs go into a down from a sit, and then there is a collapsed down, where the dog goes directly into a down from a standing position. The latter, collapsed down is my preference for when you are teaching down to your dog as a trick. I prefer the collapsed down instead of the sit-to-down behavior because it makes for a smoother, more polished look with the finished behavior. This doesn't matter so much if you're just asking your dog to "down." But it starts to matter more if perhaps you have an interest in competition obedience sports, but also for a number of other tricks to look smooth as you teach them.

- To begin teaching down, you'll take a treat and get your dog into a standing position. An easy way to do this is to toss a treat a few feet away and either go to your dog or call them back to you.

- Place the treat in front of your dog's nose so that the dog is interested. Then, move your hand with the treat down to the ground and slightly back toward their feet.

- Make sure to start with the treat on your dog's nose so they follow it down to the floor. As you move the treat back toward their feet, the dog will naturally go into a down.

- Click/treat/praise as soon as your dog's belly hits the ground.

*. When you first start, do not introduce the verbal cue "down" (or whatever you're calling the trick) until your dog is consistently following the lure into a down position. This is about you getting your handling mechanics right. When you begin using the word "down," you'll use it right as your dog's belly touches the ground, when you are already sure they will be going into the down position.

*. After a couple of training sessions, you can begin to offer the verbal cue before your dog is fully in the down, but you are confident that they are in the process of going down—you want to help keep your dog successful, so don't give the verbal cue too soon when he is learning!

*. As you begin to phase out the lure into the down position, you can start introducing more of the verbal and/or physical cues (I use a flat hand sideways). If you find that your dog isn't consistent, it's a good time to back up and go back to the lure, to make sure that your dog is able to be consistent before moving forward. Put in lots of practice at home and in low-level, mildly distracting situations before asking your dog to "down" in the park. Don't get frustrated with them—just because they "know it" at home, that doesn't mean they will automatically be able to perform it to the same level in more distracting environments. It's our job to build up to that with consistent, fun practice!

Tricks to Teach

# 3

# Sit Pretty

# 3. Sit Pretty

This trick involves your dog going into a sit position, and balancing on their hips with their front paws up in the air. Some people refer to this position as "begging." Some dogs, especially a lot of small dogs and terriers, take to this trick very quickly, and may even offer this behavior naturally. For other dogs, it might take a little bit of time for them to be able to do this trick consistently, and to be stable doing it for any length of time. Sit pretty is a trick that requires a lot of core muscle strength. Teach this trick slowly by starting with very short training sessions and recognizing that your dog may have to build muscle tone to be able to perform the trick.

- With your dog in a sit, bring a high-value treat to their nose and slowly raise the treat above their head.

- Your dog will follow the treat, raising their body up onto their hips. Click/praise and give your dog the treat!

- Start slowly. Add in the verbal cue only when your dog can consistently be lured into the sit pretty position. Click/praise and treat right when your dog gets into the position. Go very slow with building duration on this trick. Remember that your dog's core muscles are getting a big workout, and it may take some time for them to be able to hold any duration with this trick.

## Safety Note

If you have a young dog, especially a large breed dog, you'll want to talk with your veterinarian before starting to teach this trick, because it can be hard on developing joints.

## Tips

If your dog is going up onto their hind legs instead of staying on their haunches when you lure up, your hand position is probably just slightly too high. Try lowering the treat, keeping it right on your dog's nose and reward right when they get into the position you want.

Daisy shows off her sit pretty.

Photo credit: Christa Tucker

## Paw Tricks–Three Variations

These are some of my favorite tricks to teach dogs. They are relatively easy, cute, and can be especially good for urban dogs, who might have to deal with seeing neighbors in elevators, doormen, etc. These tricks, especially "wave," are very disarming to people who might not be very comfortable being around dogs, and who especially might not be excited to find themselves in an enclosed space location (like an elevator or hallway) with a dog.

# 4
—
# High-Five

# 4. High-Five

* Take a treat that your dog is excited about. For this trick, it really helps to have treats that are smelly. You want to have your dog in front of you, either in a sit or a down (sit will make it easier). Put the treat in one hand, close the hand into a fist, and hold your fist out to your dog.

* Wait! Don't get impatient with this part of the learning process. The first few times you play this game, it might take a little while for your dog to get the idea—that's okay! You want them to start using their brain, and this is a trick we aren't going to teach by luring.

* Your dog will likely start to nose at your fist, trying to figure out how to get the treat—ignore this. You don't want to discourage the behavior, but you don't want to reward it either.

* After a little bit, your dog, in an attempt to get the treat, will start to paw at your hand—jackpot! You want to click/praise/open your hand and treat your dog!

* Right now, your dog has no idea why they got the treat, but with a few repetitions, they will start to put the pieces together, figuring out that by pawing at your hand, they can get it.

* When your dog is consistently pawing at your closed fist with the treat in it, start introducing the verbal cue you want for the trick. I use "high five," but you can use anything you think is cute: "gimme some" or "lay it on me" are another couple of possible cues for this trick.

* When your dog is consistent, hold up your fist—this time without a treat in it—and cue your dog to give you five, then click/praise/treat your dog!

* Next, when your dog is consistent at offering the trick to an empty, closed fist, hold your hand out flat to them, as though you were giving a high-five to a person, and give the verbal cue. When your dog's paw touches your hand, click/treat/praise. Have a big party!

# 5
## Wave

# 5. Wave

* Once your dog knows the previous "high five" trick, waving can easily be taught using similar methods and building on the skills they have already pieced together.

* Have treats ready and hold your hand up in front of your dog like you would for a high five, but this time hold it just slightly farther away from them.

* When your dog reaches their paw up toward you, click/praise and come in right away with a treat. Repeat this step several times.

* When your dog is consistently pawing at the air with your hand just out of reach, introduce your verbal marker. I use "wave" or (when I'm feeling extra) "wave to the people" with my own dogs. And you can start to adjust the positioning of your physical cue to be even farther away. I like to wave my flat-palmed hand from side to side, as though I were waving at crowds on the side of a parade.

* Don't forget to treat your dog for a job well done, and keep practicing "high five" so your dog remembers and understands that these are two (related but) different tricks.

Mary Hostetter's dog Swag says hello with a wave.

# 6

## Shake

# 6. Shake

* Teaching your dog to shake hands is going to look similar to teaching high five, except we will change the orientation of our hand and be asking for prolonged contact. Start by taking a treat that your dog is excited about and holding your close-fisted hand in front of your dog with your hand horizontal.

* Be patient! As with high five, you want to wait and let your dog puzzle out what behavior you are looking for. This method of teaching is called shaping—you are allowing your dog to figure out the trick in small pieces before putting the finished trick together.

* Your dog may sniff at or lick your hand trying to get to the treat. Just ignore this—don't scold or punish them. As hard as it is, try to remain quiet at this point and let your dog think. It's really tempting to try to help our dogs, but unfortunately what ends up happening is that we flood them with information they don't need. Our dogs are smart! Sometimes we just need to let them puzzle out the new behavior.

* When your dog paws at your hand to try to get the treat, click/praise and immediately give them the treat.

* When your dog is consistently pawing at your closed fist with the treat in it, start introducing the verbal cue you want for the trick. I use "shake," but you can use anything, like "say hello," "introduce yourself," etc.

* When your dog is consistent, hold up your fist—this time without a treat in it—and cue your dog to shake, using whatever verbal marker you have chosen. Then click/praise/treat your dog when their paw lands on your hand!

* Next, when your dog is consistent at offering the trick to a closed fist, hold your hand out flat to your dog, as though you wanted to shake their paw, and give the verbal cue. When their paw touches your hand, click/treat/praise and have a big party!

## Tip

As with any trick, when you bring the trick out into the world and a more distracting environment, your dog might be a little slower to respond and need a higher rate of reward. This may also be true if someone else is asking your dog to do a trick like shaking their hand.

# 7

# Touch (Hand Target)

# 7. Touch (Hand Target)

This trick is one that a lot of dogs find really fun. Not necessarily the most impressive-looking trick, but one that is really versatile, this can be easy to use for dogs who might be stressed or lacking confidence in new situations, and a skill that can be used to build other tricks. The goal of the touch trick is for your dog to touch their nose to your hand, no matter where your hand is. One of my dogs knows it as "touch," my youngest dog knows it as "boop"—you can of course use any word you want as your verbal cue.

This trick involves something known as targeting. There are multiple kinds of targeting your dog can be taught to do—in this case, it's a nose target to your hand. You can also teach your dog to nose target onto objects, or to target their front feet (we will learn this later) or rear feet onto an object that you present to them, or even to target different parts of their body (cheeks, chin, hips, etc.) to your hand or an object. Once you get the basics for teaching targeting down, it's easy to expand.

This is another trick where we are going to let our dogs figure it out with our support, but without luring or direct guidance from us.

*  Hold your hand palm first in front of your dog. Have treats ready, but don't have anything in the hand that you want your dog to "target."

*  When your dog sniffs your hand, click/praise and treat!

*  Repeat this several times, praising and/or clicking and giving your dog a treat each time they sniff or nose at your hand.

*  At first, your dog might be very gentle. As they becomes more confident with what you are asking for, you can begin rewarding when they push against your hand, and not when they just lightly sniff it.

*  At this point, when your dog is targeting your hand in a way that you like, you can start adding your verbal cue.

* Begin moving your hand around—lower, higher, and side to side. Keep your hand at a level your dog can safely reach, but have it in a different position each time you ask your dog to target, so they not only are doing the targeting behavior, but having to orient themselves to where your hand is.

## Taking Targeting to the Next Level

* If you want your dog to nose target onto other objects, you can use the same method. An easy way to do this with small objects is to hold them in your hand and ask your dog to "touch" (or whatever your verbal cue is).

* You can also put a sticky note on your hand and begin by asking your dog to touch that, then move the sticky note to other locations, show it to your dog and ask them to "touch" or "target" that sticky note. Helping your dog to generalize this behavior can be a bit confusing at the start, so make sure that they have a solid understanding of the targeting behavior before generalizing to other objects. Go slowly, with lots of praise and lots of treats—remember this is new and complicated for your dog!

# 8

# Target on the Ground

# 8. Target on the Ground

A different kind of targeting is to have your dog learn how to target their feet (either front or back feet) onto an object of your choosing. You can pick any kind of "target" you want for this. Lids from large plastic yogurt containers make great training tools; you can also use Tupperware lids, box lids, and towels. My favorite items to use for ground targeting are foam baseball bases I get from the dollar store or the dollar section of many "big-box" retailers in the spring and summer. I find these bases really convenient, and I like that they aren't slick and hold up really well to dogs' targeting over time.

- To start, pull out treats and put a couple onto the container lid or whatever you're using as a target.

- Your dog will investigate the treats. When their front feet touch the target, click/praise as they eats the treats.

- Repeat several times. You want your dog to be comfortable putting their feet onto the target. Depending on what you are using as a target and how confident your dog is with different footing, some dogs might be more or less sensitive to this stage and may need more practice.

- When your dog is comfortable with their feet on the target, start adding in your cue word. My dogs know putting their front feet onto something as "target," but you can use any word you want. As your dog puts their feet onto the object you have them targeting onto, click (if you are clicker training) or praise, and then begin adding in the verbal cue. Right as their feet get on it, say "Yes! Target!" and give them treats while they are still standing on the target object.

- Next, put the treat onto the target. Holding your dog back a few inches from the target, release them and say "go target." Click/praise as your dog's feet touch the target and they get the treats.

- When your dog is comfortable with the above steps, ask them to target without a treat on the target. Set them up in front of the target, say "go target," and click/praise and treat when your puppy puts their feet onto the target.

*◦ This is a trick that a lot of dogs really enjoy and can pick up really quickly. As your dog gets more familiar, they may start to offer the targeting trick when they see the target object you train with come out. This is a great opportunity to teach your dog that tricks are fun because it's a game you play together. They only get treats/praise when you ask them to target!

## Extra Credit

In the future, you can change the object you want your dog to target. Show an object to your dog, place a treat on it, and say "target" as your dog gets the treat. Then practice targeting as you would with an object your dog is familiar with. I like to practice targeting on a variety of objects: phone books, paper plates, takeout container lids, etc., so that it is a trick behavior that my dogs are comfortable generalizing to new objects, and then to those objects in new places.

# 9

## Go To

# 9. Go To

In some ways similar to teaching your dog to target with their front feet, with this trick you are teaching your dog to move away from you and go to a location. The most practical application of this trick is to teach your dog to go to their bed, or a platform like an ottoman.

* Teaching this trick will be a bit like playing a game with your dog. First decide what object you want to send them to (bed, towel, yoga mat, etc.) and what you want to call it ("place," "bed," "spot," etc.).

* Take a treat your dog is really excited by and get next to them but a few feet away from the location you want to send your dog to. Show them the treat and, using an upbeat voice, move quickly toward the bed or other location.

* When your dog follows you and gets up onto the bed/mat, drop the treat onto the bed for them to eat. Praise with "good job! Good spot/ place/bed," etc.

* Once you've done this a couple of times and you're confident your dog is going to follow you to the bed, start to add a verbal cue as you are in motion, but continue to walk with them, gently tossing the treat as you get to the spot and your dog is already on it.

* Next, you'll put the treat on the bed or mat and walk your dog gently away by the collar. Hold them back with an arm in front of their chest to "rev 'em up," gently keeping them from moving forward, saying "ready? ready?" and then, when they are pulling toward the bed (where the treat is), let them go and say "okay!" (or whatever other release word you have). As your dog moves toward the bed, when you are confident they will continue to the spot to get the treat, say "go place/spot/bed" (whatever word you have chosen). When your dog gets onto the bed, click and praise.

*᠅* As your dog gets confident with this trick, after a few repetitions, you can begin to phase out having the treat on the bed ahead of time and just toss the treat to your dog when they go to their bed.

## Extra Credit

Teach your dog the names of different locations you want to send them to: their bed, a yoga mat, their crate, your bed, etc. Start the same way as if you were teaching for the first time and introduce new verbal markers for each location.

## Tips

Remember we want to keep this trip fast-moving, upbeat, and fun! You want your dog to be driving toward the bed, not slowly walking up, resigned to obey. If your dog starts slowing down, go back a step, start running with your dog toward the bed again, or placing treats on the bed, revving your dog up, and encouraging them to move quickly toward the bed. You want to keep this fun!

# 10

## Two On/Paws Up

# 10. Two On/Paws Up

For this trick, your dog is going to be putting their two front feet onto an object that you select. Remember it's your responsibility to pick objects that can safely support your dog. This trick is fun for having your dog pose for pictures, is a good foundation skill, and builds core muscle as well as rear foot awareness. Paws up is also really useful if you have any interest in exploring the sport of canine parkour.

When starting with this trick, your dog may initially try to fully jump with all four feet onto the object, so it's helpful to go slow and help them to understand what you want.

- To start, I like to use a one-step step stool that you can get at the dollar store, or a upside down water bowl. At first, you want something very sturdy that won't move under your dog's feet.

- Take a high-level treat and position your dog in front of the object you are asking them to paw up onto. Position the treat right above your dog's nose, and move it up and forward.

- In order to get to the treat, your dog will put their front paws up on the object. Click/praise and give your dog the treat!

As your dog becomes more familiar with the trick, you can experiment with different heights of objects.

Photo credit: Kathleen Tepperies

*❋* Lure your dog a few more times with the treat in front of their nose. When they are confidently putting their feet onto the object, start saying "paws up" as your dog moves their front feet onto the object and while still eating the treat. Timing is important! You want to make sure they knows they are getting the treat for being in the right position.

*❋* After a few training sessions combining the treat lure and the verbal cue when your dog is in position, put them in front of the object you have been practicing with and ask them to "paws up." If they do, click/praise/treat and have a little party!

## Extra Credit

*❋* As your dog gets more familiar with this trick, you can challenge them by asking them to paw up on more challenging surfaces, smaller objects, or moving objects (that are stable and won't hurt your dog). This is one of my favorite things to practice with my dogs. I sometimes will do thirty-day paws-up challenges where every day I'll ask my dogs to paw up onto a new object, either at home or in the world, to build confidence.

*❋* You can also ask your dog to put their feet onto (safe) things that may move (example: exercise ball, hammock, rope strung between two sturdy objects). Start slowly with this and bring out lots of treats. Many dogs, especially large dogs, are understandably cautious about putting their feet onto something that might move.

# 11

---

# Say Your Prayers/
# Head Duck

# 11. Say Your Prayers/Head Duck

*. Ask your dog to "paws up," using your two paws up cue, onto your outstretched arm. If your dog is nervous or uncertain about putting their paws up onto you, you can lure with a treat to start.

*. When your dog has both paws up on your arm, take a treat in your other hand and put it under your arm.

*. When your dog's nose dips between their two legs up on your arm, praise, treat, and release them.

*. Add in the verbal cue. "Prayers" or "say your prayers" are the most common, but some less religious options include "shy" and "hide."

*. As your dog becomes more familiar with the behavior, you can phase out of having the treat under your arm and just give the treat when your dog completes the trick.

*. If your dog drops one of their paws in the process of ducking their head under, don't worry, that's normal. Just start over-rewarding when both feet are up on your arm and your dog's head drops.

# 12
## Four On

## 12. Four On

For this trick, you will be teaching your dog to fully get onto an object, like a small platform or table. This trick is excellent for beginning to teach your dog how to use and think about rear feet placement. Dogs are for the most part front-wheel-drive animals, the back feet follow where the front feet go, and we have to specifically teach our dogs to be thoughtful about where they put their back feet.

Lenore Pawlowski's Leia practicing "four on" on some playground equipment.

* Find a relatively small platform that you are confident has enough room for your dog to get up onto. There are commercially available platforms like the one made by "KLIMB," but you can also use many things you might have around the house, like an ottoman or a step stool (depending on your dog's size). The most important thing is that the object is sturdy and not too high. We want something the dog can comfortably climb up onto without having to jump.

* Take a treat and lure your dog up onto the platform. Your dog will likely follow the treat. They may offer the two-paws-up previously taught—that's okay. Don't give them the cookie; hold it just out of reach and continue to encourage.

- When your dog's four feet are on the platform, click/praise and give the treat right away.

- Before your dog jumps/steps off, give them their release word.

- You want the platform to be a fun place for your dog. As you work the trick more, you can continue to offer treats while your dog elects to stay on the platform. When your dog gets off, there's no correction or chastising—the treats just stop coming. Soon your dog will be wanting to "stick" to the platform because it's a place where really good things happen, a.k.a. they are being fed treats.

- When your dog is comfortable getting up onto the platform with the lure, you can begin to phase that out, giving the verbal cue for platform. Some examples include "place," "up," "platform," or anything else that makes sense to you, right before the dog is about to get on.

- Before your dog gets off, be sure to give them their release command, so they understand you want them to get up on something and stay there.

Extra Credit: Work slowly toward your dog balancing on your body like Corinne Andersen's Topo.

## Extra Credit

*. Take this trick on the road! How many objects can you find on your walk for your dog to get up onto? Rocks, (stable) logs, and other things like park benches are great places to reinforce this trick outside of your living room.

*. How small an object can your dog (safely) get all four feet onto? This is a skill you can continue to develop over time, as your dog gets more familiar with their foot placement.

*. Next, work on objects that might move slightly, but are still safe. Start slowly with this; moving objects can be very worrying for dogs. Fun examples include small wagons, pool floats (make sure this is supervised and that your dog knows how to swim!), agility teeters, etc.

# 13
# Go Under

# 13. Go Under

Depending on how flexible you are, this trick is easiest with small dogs, but can be done with larger dogs as well—it just might require more creativity with finding or making objects for your dog to go under. Note: the lower they have to go to get under the object, the harder it's going to be. Try to start with objects that they have to just slightly duck to get under, and then progress to lower objects once your dog is familiar with the trick.

- ❖ Sit on the floor and bend your knees like a bridge. Get some treats your dog is excited about and ask them to down next to you, facing your bent knees. (If you don't want to teach this trick with your legs, you can also teach it using an object in the world, like a park bench or a bike lock stand on the sidewalk. For those objects, your dog likely won't need to be lying down.)

- ❖ Put the treat right in front of your dog's nose and pull them forward. Go very slowly so that your dog is more inclined to start to crawl or duck (depending on the height of the object) instead of getting up to try to get the treat.

- ❖ When your dog's back is under your knees (or whatever object you are asking them to go under), toss the cookie gently forward to encourage your dog to crawl the rest of the way through and move forward.

- ❖ Repeat and begin adding in the verbal cue that you want to use for this trick. Some options include: "tunnel," "under," "through," "excavate," or anything else you can think of! As your dog begins to understand the verbal cue, you can start to phase out the physical lure. You can also begin to phase out asking your dog to down first; they will begin to understand that they need to chain behaviors together by lying down in order to go under your legs!

## Extra Credit

This is also a great trick that can translate well to canine parkour skills, if that is a sport/activity you and your dog are interested in exploring. On your walks, try to find different (safe and stable) objects that you can ask your dog to go under. To be challenging, they don't have to be especially low; just the act of going under something is a new experience for many dogs. This trick will also prepare your dog well for the tunnel, if you ever want to test their agility.

Thyra Powers' Ozzie going through an agility tunnel.

# 14
## Crawl

# 14. Crawl

This is a trick that can help to increase your dog's physical strength; it's one of the first exercises that my dog Sirius' physical therapist started her on after she had reconstructive surgery on both of her knees.

* Start by getting your dog into a down position.

* Take treats that your dog is excited about and place one a few inches in front of them.

* Encourage your dog to pull their body forward toward the treat.

* If your dog gets up, that's okay—pick up the treat, ask them to go into down position, and start again. If you pull the treat too far forward, they are more likely to stand up, so start very slow. Your goal is for them to pull themself forward just an inch or two. Remember, this is encouraging your dog to use muscles they might not have used much before; they have to figure out how to move their body.

* This trick can take a little bit of time to build up duration on. Don't give up and don't try to move too quickly. Just keep putting treats just a few inches ahead of your dog, and when they are consistently "crawling" toward the treat, you can add in the verbal cue of your choice. Then slowly fade out the treat lure by asking your dog to "crawl" and immediately clicking/praising and treating instead of putting the treats inches in front of them.

# 15
—
# Put Your Toys Away

# 15. Put Your Toys Away

If your dogs are anything like mine, they have a lot of toys! I love dog toys as much as my dogs do, but putting them away can be quite a chore. What if your dogs could help you?

- Start with a toy box that has an open top, a couple of toys that your dog likes, and some yummy treats.

- Encourage your dog to pick up the toy and then call them toward the toy bin.

- When your dog reaches the toy bin, ask them to "drop," If they do, click/praise and treat!

- If your dog is reluctant to let the toy go, show them the high-value treats in your hand and make a "trade," When they drop the toy to take the cookie, praise and treat.

- If your dog already knows the names of different toys (see page 161), you can start asking them to get specific toys and bring them to the toy bin.

- Start incorporating your verbal cue as your dog is on their way back toward the toy bin—"clean up," "tidy," or "get your toys."

## Extra Credit

This trick can be easily modified for some cute holiday tricks. For example, for Easter, get an Easter basket and some Easter-themed dog toys, like squeaky eggs or (dog-safe) plush bunnies. Scatter the toys and then ask your dog to "put those toys away" into the Easter basket! You can do the same thing with a Christmas stocking: hold the stocking open and ask your dog to stuff the stocking!

# 16

—

# Fetch to Hand

Fetch is a fun game, and it's also a trick that can be taught.

Photo credit: Kelli Whitfield

# 16. Fetch to Hand

Fetch is seen as this natural "thing" that all dogs do, but it actually isn't! I talk to so many people who feel like they are failures because their dogs can't/won't do it. Fetch is a trick, and like any other skill, it can be learned and isn't something every dog comes pre-programmed knowing how to do. My champion trick dog Charlotte has a beautiful fetch, and it's 100 percent taught. She doesn't have a natural fetch, but no one would know that by watching her retrieve. In contrast, my Newfoundland has a beautiful natural retrieve (it's a very natural thing for the breed), but her "fetch" looks just the same now as my older dog's taught retrieve. This is the trick I think I'm asked how to teach the most often, not because it's the most impressive trick, but because it's something most people want their dogs to be able to do because it's fun, and they (unfortunately) feel embarrassed if their dogs don't do it.

To teach your dog to fetch, we're going to start by slowly, breaking the trick down into tiny incremental steps.

- Start by teaching your dog to "hold" an object—using a toy your dog likes is the easiest way to start this trick (see page 101).

- When your dog is comfortable holding an object, hold the object out to your dog and ask them to take/hold it. If they take the object off your outstretched palm, click/praise and treat!

- When your dog has been successful at that step, put the object on the floor in front of him. Ask your dog to pick up the object. When they do, click/praise and treat!

- If your dog is very reluctant to hold any toy in their mouth, you can buy or make a food pouch using fun fur and a zipper, tuck treats inside, and show your dog the "toy." Drag the toy around in front of them and encourage them to chase and/or tug.

- When your dog has been successful holding and picking up the toy, you can start moving the object farther away to ask them to get the object. You'll want to really break this down and only increase the difficulty very slowly, moving the object you are asking your dog to retrieve inches away at first, instead of going from right next to you to all the way across the room in one step. This is something called thin slicing, breaking down the finished behavior into very small incremental pieces. This enables you to make sure that your dog stays successful and does not get frustrated by unclear or overly complicated criteria.

* By building distance slowly and keeping your treats very high-value, you are going to build drive in your dog even if they are a dog that doesn't have a natural retrieve. The key is being patient and not trying to go too far too fast.

* As you build the difficulty for your dog, alternate between asking them to retrieve items that you place some distance away from them, and asking them to retrieve items that you have tossed. Also, be sure to vary the objects that you are asking them to retrieve, to make sure it's a trick your dog can comfortably do with different kinds of toys.

# 17
—
# Back Up

# 17. Back Up

This is a great trick to teach any dog. It's impressive-looking and is an excellent way for your dog to build muscle tone and gain rear foot awareness. Dogs are naturally "front-wheel drive" and don't have great awareness of their rear feet until we teach them that skill. Having rear foot awareness is wonderful for trick training and life skills, and is highly transferable to other sport training you might do in the future, like agility. As with most tricks, there are different ways to teach this one, but this is the way I've found easiest for dogs of all sizes.

- Take treats your dog is excited about, that they can nibble small bits off of, like string cheese or hot dogs.

- Position your dog in front of you, standing. Get them excited about the treat, keeping it right on their nose, and allow them to gently nibble at the end of the treat.

- Slowly walk toward/into your dog, and the minute you see one rear foot move, click/praise and treat!

- Don't rush! You want to reward your dog for being slow, methodical, and thoughtful. While this trick may seem easy to you, it's complicated for the dog, and if you begin moving too quickly, they may start to hop backward quickly instead of being thoughtful about where they place their feet individually.

- This is when you want to begin adding in your verbal cue as you move toward your dog. Examples of verbal cues include "back," "beep-beep" (like a heavy vehicle backing up), and "scoot."

- As you practice, your dog will begin to anticipate the moment. Click/praise and treat! This is exactly what you want. Heavily reward individual foot movement, and begin saying the verbal cue before moving into your dog. Remember the key is to go slow—we want to reward individual foot movements, so our dog is being thoughtful about foot placements.

## Tip

If your dog is backing up very crooked, you can back them up next to a wall to help keep them straighter as they back up. Once your dog is backing up straighter, you can transition to doing the trick in a more open area. For some dogs, working on back up down a hallway can also really help.

# 18

## Ride in a Wagon

# 18. Ride in a Wagon

This trick is great for supporting dogs in being more comfortable putting their feet on other moving objects like boats and docks.
Photo credit: Kelly Ford

Teaching your dog to ride in a wagon can be a fun trick to add into a trick routine, with either you pulling the wagon or another dog pushing. This trick is often easier for the small dogs who are (generally) used to the ground moving under them because they get picked up more regularly than our large dogs, are often on couch pillows that move, etc.

Depending on the size of your dog, you may be able to find an inexpensive small wagon in the spring/summer outdoor toys section of most dollar stores.

For larger dogs, you'll need a kid-sized wagon (be sure to check weight limits). I like to always outfit the bottoms of my wagons with something non-skid, to make a dog more comfortable getting into the wagon and decreasing the likelihood of a slip, which could scare or even injure your dog.

- Pat the wagon to encourage your dog to get into the wagon. If the dog gets in, praise and treat. If they are nervous about the wagon, reward any interest in the wagon, and then for touching the wagon with any part of their body.

- Your goal is to make the wagon a very positive place to be, so one strategy for this is to give your dog small treats as long as they are staying in the wagon. When they jump out of the wagon, make getting back in part of the game, and then give more treats.

- Next, put some high-value treats into the wagon and, while your dog is eating them, start to slightly rock the wagon back and forth, praising your dog.

- Encourage your dog to get out of the wagon and give lots of praise when they do.

- Repeat, slightly increasing the distance you roll the wagon, tossing treats to your dog in of the wagon.

- Add in your verbal cue, like "get in," "wagon," or "go for a ride."

- Start to build duration with riding by praising and treating your dog for staying in the wagon as you move it.

- Soon your pup will be ready to ride in style down the hallway, star in a parade, or ride and chill on your next walk to the park.

# 19

## Peek-A-Boo

# 19. Peek-A-Boo

For this trick you will be teaching your dog to go behind you and between your legs. This is a cute trick and can also be really useful to position your dog if you are waiting in line together to go to a dog-friendly event, or if your dog is nervous around people. Having your dog between your legs is a great way to deter (all but the rudest) strangers from trying to pet your dog!

- Have your dog in front of you and have treats in both your right and left hand.

- Face your dog and lure them with your left hand toward you.

- Reach between your legs with your right hand and a treat.

- Bring your dog through your legs, stopping them with their shoulders even with your knees. Give your dog the treat and praise, then release. If your dog is reluctant to move forward, you can toss another treat forward to move them out of the peek-a-boo position.

- As your dog becomes more familiar with what you want, you can phase out the treat lure and transition to an empty hand, which will become your physical lure. You can also add in your verbal cue of choice—"middle," "peek-a-boo," and "center" are great options but, as with any trick, you can call this one whatever you want.

## Extra Credit

You can teach your dog to come into peek-a-boo position from your right side by repeating the above steps on the right side. Even though your dog might be very familiar with the trick on your left, you might need to go slowly. Also practice out on your walks—be careful not to get your dog tangled with the leash.

# 20

## Walk on Your Feet

# 20. Walk on Your Feet

Rebel practicing walking on Kathleen Tepperies's feet.

This is a more advanced version of the peek-a-boo trick. For this trick, your dog will go between your legs, put their front feet onto your feet, and together you will crab-walk forward. Hint: if you want to do this trick but have a very small dog, you may need to keep your toes pointed very close together for your dog to be able to reach each of your feet with their front feet. This trick is also challenging if you have a very large dog; my Newfoundland (giant breed) and I are physically incapable of doing this one because I am too short, and she is too tall!

- Ask your dog to come into the peek-a-boo position.

- Have treats in your hand that your dog is really excited about and point your toes toward each other (this will make it easier for your dog).

---

*۰ Lift your hand up and toward the right; with your dog's nose on the treat, you should be able to steer your dog's body by moving their head. Your goal here is to support your dog by guiding them into the position of (to start) putting their right front paw onto your right foot, or their left front paw onto your left foot. To start, just focus on getting one paw on one foot. As soon as your dog's paw gets onto your foot, click/praise and treat.

*۰ Once you are consistently able to lure your dog to put one paw onto one of your feet, start trying to get their second paw onto your second foot. Use the same lure technique of moving your dog's head (and the feet will follow) by keeping their nose on a treat, and lure them forward and up. Make sure to keep your toes pressed close together to help make it easier for your dog to get their paws onto your feet. This might take some practice because a lot of us teach our dogs not to walk on us, so some dogs will take a little bit of encouragement and practice to understand that you actually do want them to walk on you.

*۰ Once your dog is comfortably being lured onto both of your feet, you can add your verbal cue. You can call this trick anything you want. Some cute examples are "shuffle," "slippers," and "tootsies." Start by introducing the verbal cue right before your dog puts their paws up onto your feet, then click, praise and treat. Then begin verbally cuing without the lure. If at any point your dog seems to get confused or frustrated, just return to the previous step and practice that more in your training sessions, before making things a bit more difficult again.

*۰ Next, you'll start walking—well, it's more like a waddle. Start very slow, with lots of praise as you begin to just start shuffling your feet. Allow your dog to get comfortable with the feeling of your feet moving under theirs. It can help to put the food lure back on your dog's nose to more heavily reinforce, along with the verbal praise, as you begin to move your feet.

*۰ Build up the number of steps you take very slowly and start to experiment with how high you can lift your feet with your dog's paws staying on. Keep it fun and playful, lots of treats and praise!

# 21
## Hold

# 21. Hold

When you train hold, start with a toy like Glinda a.k.a. TDCH SDCH Medlee's Ruby Slippers.
Photo credit: Diana Squicciarini

The point of this trick is to be able to ask your dog to hold an object of your choosing. Make sure that you ask your dogs to hold safe things, so avoid things that your dog could choke on, or anything sharp or toxic, etc. The eventual goal with this trick is that your dog will be able to hold any object you hand her: from a pencil to a wrench to a hotdog (not kidding!). When you are starting, it helps to use objects that your dog is familiar with and knows they are allowed to have in their mouth. Plush toys and balls make great options for starting with this trick, especially if your dog enjoys playing with toys.

- Take the toy that you are going to work on asking your dog to hold. You'll also want some high-value treats, and a clicker (if you clicker train). TIP: If your dog is struggling with grasping what you want, or you are teaching a dog who isn't especially toy-motivated, you can start this trick using a dog chew, like a bone or bully-stick type treat, that your dog wants to put in their mouth!

- Sit or stand with your dog facing you and show the object to your dog.

- When your dog sniffs or goes to investigate the object, click/praise and treat. At this stage, you want to reward any interest in the object.

- Next, start looking for more interest before rewarding, so instead of clicking (or verbally marking) when your dog sniffs the toy, wait until they put their mouth onto the toy, then immediately click (or verbally mark), praise, and treat.

- Once your dog is putting their mouth regularly onto the toy, you want to start adding duration into the trick by not immediately clicking/praising your dog's mouth hitting the toy, but incrementally increasing the parameters for what gets rewarded. So, to start, you are rewarding the instant your dog's mouth hits the toy; next, you want to increase to maybe half a second, and then a second. This is where you can add in your verbal cue: "hold" and "take" are two common verbal cues.

- You want to go very slowly with this trick. Trying to push for too much too quickly will confuse your dog and may result in the trick being a little less consistent.

- Once your dog is keeping their mouth on the object until you click/praise/treat, you can start adding in more time and begin very slowly moving your hands off the object you are asking your dog to hold. Start with just a fraction of a second, then put your hands back on the object so your dog doesn't drop it. Praise your dog—"good hold"—take the object, and give them a treat.

- Each training session, you can begin slowly increasing the time increments that you're asking your dog to hold an object. You can praise and remind your dog "good hold" while they are holding to reinforce the behavior that you want.

❋ Always be sure to put your hands back onto the object before releasing your dog, to keep the object from dropping. This is also a good time to start diversifying the objects that you ask your dog to hold. If you started with a tennis ball, ask your dog to hold a plush toy, an empty paper towel tube, a capped pen, etc. Experiment with different textures and weights (but stay away from anything super heavy).

Hold is a very versatile trick—once your dog gets good at it, they can hold almost anything (don't worry, the knife isn't real)!

Photo credit: Kelli Whitfield

# 22
---
# Leave It

Kelli Whitfield's dogs practicing Leave It.

# 22. Leave It

This is a trick that both is impressive and can literally save your dog's life if they are looking toward something that could hurt them. Especially for city dogs, teaching a dog to ignore things on the ground can really help keep them safe from trash hazards.

- Take two treats, put one in your fist, and present it to your dog. At first your dog is going to do lots of things to try to get at the treat, sniffing, licking, pawing, etc. Ignore all of this; this is the hard part. Don't discourage, just ignore them.

- After not being successful, your dog will pull back. In that moment, click/praise, say "good leave it!" (or whatever another verbal cue you use), and give the second treat—NOT the one in your fist hand.

- As you practice, again, when your dog ignores the treat in your fist, say "yes! leave it" and give the other treat to them. You don't want to confuse your dog when they are first learning by giving the treat that you have just told them to ignore.

- As your dog gets better at the game, start keeping the treat you want them to leave on your palm instead of in a closed fist. Tell your dog "leave it" and praise as they do! If your dog goes for the treat, just close your hand around the first one and play the game using the previous steps again until your dog is more confident.

- When your dog is comfortably playing the game with leaving treats in your hand, start putting treats on the ground. Start with treats next to you, so that you can step on the treat and prevent your dog from getting it if they aren't quite ready for that level. If at any point your dog struggles with this trick, just go back to earlier steps and play at that level until your dog is consistently successful, then move onto the next level.

# 23

# Drop It

# 23. Drop It

This is a trick that builds on the earlier trick of asking your dog to hold an item (page 101). Now you need to get it back from your dog! To begin this trick, start with an object in your dog's mouth, either an object that you have asked your dog to hold, or if your dog is very toy-motivated, you can start work on this trick while they are playing with a toy.

* Have a very high-value treat that your dog is excited about.

* While your dog has the toy or other object in their mouth show them the treat. As your dog leaves the toy for the treat, say "yes!" or click and give them the treat.

* This isn't about bribing the dog, this is about paying your dog for doing something very unnatural to them, dropping something that they actively want in their mouth. This might be a toy, but in the future, a real-world application of this trick might be a chicken bone from the sidewalk, which could be very dangerous if swallowed. Drop it is a hard trick for dogs that doesn't come naturally. We need to pay them for their labor, and we want our dogs to understand that when we ask them to do something hard, we always have something better.

* Very quickly you can start to add in the verbal marker, right as the toy drops from your dog's mouth: "drop," "bye," "fall," and "give" are all good verbal marker options for this trick. Then start to say "drop" (or whatever cue you choose) right as you pull out the treat and show it to your dog. When your dog is successful at this level, start to cue the behavior without showing your dog the treat—just don't forget to pay your dog after they complete the trick!

# 24

---

# Pick Up

# 24. Pick Up

This trick is very versatile (and can even be practical). You want your dog to pick up any object that you indicate. If your dog already knows "hold," this will be easier, but dogs don't generalize well, so picking an object up, say, off the ground or the sofa will be an added challenge for many dogs.

Choose an item you would like to start teaching your dog to pick up (once they are familiar with the trick you can generalize this to anything else you would like your dog to carry). I recommend starting with a ball or toy your dog is comfortable putting in their mouth.

* Get your dog's attention and put the toy/item down in front of them. Have some high-value treats ready. When your dog approaches the toy, click/praise and reward. If your dog is very toy-motivated, you might choose to wait until your dog puts the toy in their mouth; if your dog is less sure about toys, click/praise reward for any interest in the toy/item.

* Start to build up the criteria that your dog needs to follow in order to get the treats, so you'll be waiting for your dog to put their mouth on the toy for the first round (if you initially started with just rewarding for sniffing). When your dog puts their mouth on the toy, it's likely the toy will come slightly off the floor. Click/praise/treat. You can at this time start adding in the verbal cue for this trick. Common options include "get," "pick up," and "grab."

* Practice, practice, practice, increasing the criteria, making sure your dog is actually picking up the item, not just nosing at it. At this point, you can start to ask your dog to pick up different items. Start with different toys and items your dog is already comfortable putting in their mouth, and then expand to other items you would like your dog to pick up for you.

## Extra Credit

Ask your dog to bring an item to you. This will involve combining picking up an object, carrying, and retrieving. Putting multiple skills like this together is called chained behavior. Start very close to your dog and then start adding distance.

# 25
## Over

## 25. Over

This is a really versatile trick. It's great if you are thinking you might want to do dog sports, like competition obedience, rally obedience, agility, or flyball, with your dog. The goal of this trick is to support your dog in becoming comfortable with stepping and then jumping over an object that you indicate. You can make a jump using a broomstick, an empty wrapping-paper tube and books, or a plastic storage container. The goal is to find something to use as a jump that is light, so it won't startle or hurt your dog if they jump into it or the bar falls.

## Safety First

This trick is not about seeing how high you can get your dog to jump. Jumping puts a lot of strain onto your dog's joints. It's always a good idea to talk with your veterinarian before starting to teach your dog to jump, especially if your dog is young, older, overweight, or has ever had joint issues.

* Start by setting up the "jump" you want your dog to go over. Again, we aren't looking for height here—one or two inches off the ground is plenty to start, even for large dogs.

* Put your dog next to you in front of the jump.

* Without showing your dog the treat (we want them to look at the jump, not at your hand, for safety reasons, so they are focusing on where their body is, not on looking at you), toss the treat over the jump. Try to toss it about one and a half to two body-lengths past the jump, which ensures that your dog has plenty of room to safely get over it.

* As your dog follows the treat over the jump, click/praise and allow them to get the treat.

* Repeat a few times, throwing the treat over the jump, and begin adding in your preferred verbal cue—"jump" and "over" are both popular options. Start introducing the verbal cue just as your dog has committed to the jump. If your dog tries to go around the jump to get the treat, that's okay! Just get the treat before they get to it.

* As you throw the treat, remember to try to keep your dog from watching your hand. Just toss the treat from the hand farthest from your dog, so they are looking at the jump and see the treat fall ahead of them.

* As your dog becomes more familiar with the jump, you can start adding multiple jumps together, creating a little indoor-agility "jumpers" course for your dog. You can also start to slightly increase the jump height. Again, it's always a good idea to talk with your veterinarian before asking your dog to jump any kind of height. You also want to make sure that your jump is on a safe surface. Do not ask your dog to jump on hardwood or any other kind of hard or slippery floors—this is to protect your dog's joints.

When thinking about safety of jump heights, I think it's useful to look at how heights are approached with dog agility. For agility competitions, the height a dog jumps is determined by their height at the withers (shoulders). There are a variety of agility organizations and they each have their own jump heights. For some perspective, below is the most updated jump height for American Kennel Club (AKC) agility. I would treat these as a maximum jump height, but raise the height (no higher than this) slowly. Again, these are maximum jump heights for dogs who are healthy and in good physical condition.

Barb Wright's Sophie jumping in an agility competition.

Jump height of 8 inches: For dogs 11 inches and under at the withers.

Jump height of 12 inches: For dogs 14 inches and under at the withers.

Jump height of 16 inches: For dogs 18 inches and under at the withers.

Jump height of 20 inches: For dogs 22 inches and under at the withers.

Jump height of 24 inches: For dogs over 22 inches at the withers.

Young dogs, older dogs, or dogs with pre-existing medical conditions should not jump these heights, and healthy dogs need to work up to them. It's always a good idea to consult with a veterinarian before beginning any jumping.

# 26

---

# Jump Over
# My Leg/Arm

# 26. Jump Over My Leg/Arm

Jumping over your arms is an impressive trick sure to please any crowd.
Photo credit: Chrissy Joy

Tricks that involve your dog interacting with your body are a real crowd-pleaser. They are fun, especially because you don't need any props, making them ideal tricks if you live in a small space or to bring on the road.

- Start by getting on the ground with your dog and, similar to how you set them up to go over a "jump," put your leg straight out flat on the ground, toss a treat and give your dog's verbal jump cue. Praise/click and treat when your dog goes over!

*. After a few repetitions, start to raise your leg a bit higher, but don't go too high. Keep in mind the jump height maximum suggestions for jumps (on page 115).

*. When your dog is successful with leg jumps while you are on the ground, sit on a chair, put your leg out and cue the dog. If they are struggling, you can toss a treat again to help remind them. If your dog is going around your leg, try doing this trick with your foot against a wall at first, to keep your dog from going around it. When they are consistently successful, try moving away from the wall slowly.

*. Teaching your dog to jump over your arm may be trickier for your dog (and your own flexibility!). I start with this trick also on the ground, either sitting or lying (depending on the size of your dog). Put your arm out like a jump bar, toss a treat with your other hand, and give your dog the verbal jump cue.

*. Gradually work up to bending over with your arm out. Many dogs are nervous about you bending over them, so crouching instead of bending at the waist may help with teaching your dog to jump over your arm.

Tricks to Teach

Rebel jumping through Kathleen Tepperies' arms.

## Extra Credit

As your dog gets better with this trick, you can make it a bit harder by expanding into having your dog jump through your circled arms. Start slowly to curl your arm and then reach your other arm over to create an oval. Obviously, this trick is dependent upon your dog being small enough to fit through your arms! Start slow and low. If bending over is difficult or uncomfortable for you, try lying on the ground.

# 27
---
# Jump Into My Arms

# 27. Jump Into My Arms

This is one of my favorite tricks. For this trick, your dog will jump into your arms or, depending on the size of the dog, run up your body and into your arms. Before starting to teach this trick, like jumping, you will want to make sure that your dog is physically capable of learning it. You'll also want to take your own physical health and strength into consideration, as well as the size of your dog. Not all tricks are right for every dog! For most people, this trick is best for small to medium-sized dogs. For example, it's definitely not something that I'm going to teach my Newfoundland!

My first agility dog (a Miniature Schnauzer) loved this trick, and it's how we would end all of our competition agility runs, with him jumping into my arms as we exited the ring after we crossed the finish line.

*۰ To start with this trick, you'll want your dog to be comfortable being on your body. With puppies, many of us teach our dogs to not walk on our bodies, so your dog will need to get more comfortable doing this.

*۰ Start on the ground (if your dog is small) or sit on a chair without arms if you have a medium-sized (or larger) dog. Encourage your dog to jump into your lap. Do this by patting your lap, lots of encouragement, kissy noises, whatever gets them excited. When your dog jumps into your lap, praise/click and treat!

*۰ When your dog is comfortably jumping into your lap, remove the chair and crouch (this is good exercise for you!) and encourage your dog to jump into your lap, just the same way you did when you had a chair supporting you, but as you are crouching, keep one leg positioned out in front of you. This gives your dog something to brace themselves on as they make the climb up into your arms.

*   As your dog gets better at this, you can begin crouching less, bending backward, but being sure to keep your leg out to give your dog something to aim toward and "run up" your body.

*   Keep this trick fun for your dog and don't do a lot of repetitions. Remember this is a physically strenuous trick for your dog, especially if they haven't done a lot of jumping. Be sure to always practice this trick on supportive footing (carpet, grass, matting, etc.), not hardwood floors or concrete.

# 28
# Basketball

# 28. Basketball

This trick is my dog Charlotte's favorite! For this trick, your dog will take a ball of your choosing and dunk it into a small basketball hoop. You will need some props for this trick. Children's basketball hoops can be found at any toy store, or even at most dollar stores. You can find small folding hoops which work really well.

Pam Regan AKC judge's trick dog, stunt dog, and breed champion, Belgian Tervuren, playing basketball.

* For this trick, you'll be combining tricks we worked on earlier, like "hold" and "drop." We will also be adding in some new skills that involve your dog putting the ball in a specific place: in this case, the basketball hoop.

* If your dog tends to be nervous about new things, show your dog the hoop and offer a treat. This will help your dog make positive associations with the hoop.

* Ask your dog to hold the ball and put the basketball hoop in front of their face. This is easiest if you start with a dollar-store-type hoop that you can hold in your hand, so your dog doesn't have to go far, then ask your dog to drop the ball. Click/praise and treat!

- Begin adding in your verbal cue (I use "make a basket," but you can use anything like "basketball," "rimshot," "slam dunk"). After a few repetitions, your dog will begin to understand that the goal is to put the ball into the hoop. Remember this trick is quite tricky and involves your dog needing to understand complicated behaviors put together. Aiming the ball into the hoop can be especially challenging for some dogs.

- Keep your training sessions short and fun! This is one that dogs can get frustrated with quickly if they aren't quite understanding. If your dog isn't consistently making the basket, go back a step and move the basketball closer to your dog to help them to be successful when you are teaching.

## Extra Credit

- Instead of handing your dog the ball, begin asking them to pick the ball up and make a basket.

- Start with the ball right in front of your dog so they don't have to go anywhere. Over time, you can build up to throwing a ball or asking your dog to go get it from a distance and come and dunk it in the hoop.

# 29
—
# Speak

# 29. Speak

This is a trick that I like to teach by a method called "capturing." This means you will teach your dog to do this trick on cue by rewarding your dog and putting a cue onto a behavior they do naturally. I find this trick much easier to teach using a clicker because it makes it easy to mark a very specific thing that your dog is doing easier/faster than if I use verbal cues.

- Have your clicker and treats ready. You can either wait for your dog to bark naturally, or you can do something that will elicit a bark (like ringing the doorbell, making strange noises, etc.).

- When your dog barks, click, praise, and treat!

- This is a trick that most dogs pick up fairly quickly, so you can start introducing your verbal cue right away. Pick your verbal cue early, such as "talk," "speak," "bark," "yell," etc. You can also get a bit more creative if you want to use the trick, say, in conversation with your dog. My youngest puppy knows both "speak" and "please" to mean she should bark, so I can say "say please" and she will bark—it's very cute. After you make the noise that is going to get your dog to bark, and as your dog starts to bark, say "good speak," or whatever verbal cue you want, and immediately click and treat. We are trying to mark a singular bark and then interrupt the barking with a treat so your dog will begin to understand that what you are looking for is a bark, not a frenzied chorus of barks.

- After a few repetitions, when you think your dog is catching on, try saying your verbal cue immediately before making a sound that cues barking to your dog. Click/praise and treat.

- Next, get your dog's attention and say the verbal cue; if your dog barks, jackpot! Lots of praise, lots of treats! If they don't bark, go back a step for a few practice sessions. Your dog will be chatting in no time!

## Extra Credit

As counterintuitive as it sounds, teaching your dog to "speak" on cue can actually support you with decreasing unwanted barking. When you teach your dog to speak on cue, treat and then praise your dog for "quiet." Very quickly, your dog will begin to understand the difference between the two, and you'll be able to ask your dog politely to stop yelling at the squirrel out the window! I like to use "thank you" as a verbal cue for asking my dogs to stop barking.

# 30
---
# Scratch Art

# 30. Scratch Art

This is a great trick for the crafty dog in your life. It's one of my favorite tricks to teach because not only is it cute, it's not messy, and it also comes with a souvenir at the end that you can put up on the refrigerator or gift to friends and family, and who doesn't want a gift made for them by a doggo?!

For this trick you will need to get some of the special "scratch art" paper. You can find this relatively inexpensively at any craft store or online. The paper starts out matte black, and then under the matte is either different-colored or glittery underlayers. Usually scratch art paper comes with little stick styluses to draw on it, but for this trick you won't need those, your doggo is going to be doing all the art!

- I like to take a piece of the scratch art paper and attach it to something stable like a clipboard, or a binder. You can use masking or washi tape to affix the edges to the hard surface.

- Have yummy treats ready and ask your dog to "high five" to remind them about that trick. Do a few repetitions, praise/click and treat.

- Next, position the scratch art paper in front of your dog and ask for "high five." Your dog might be confused at first because we are asking them to generalize a behavior into a new situation. If they don't respond, put the paper down and ask for high five just with your hand again. When they are successful at that, bring the scratch art paper back out. When your dog's paw hits the page, click/praise and treats.

- As your dog's nails hit the page, they will make a mark by scratching off the black overlayer on the scratch art paper, revealing the colors below.

- The more you ask your dog to paw the page, the more art they will create! If your dog isn't scratching hard enough to make clear marks on the scratch art paper (it doesn't take much pressure, so even the smallest dogs can do this), you can experiment with the angle at which you hold the page.

* Remember to keep treating your dog as they "draw" on the scratch art page. You can also rotate the page to make sure that they are filling the whole page with art.

## Extra Credit

When your dog finishes a page, you can frame Doggo's masterpiece or magnet it up on the refrigerator!

# 31
# Roll Over

# 31. Roll Over

Veronica Tan's dog demonstrates that rolling over takes coordination, muscle tone, and trust for your dog.

Roll over is a classic dog trick that has passed the test of time! Roll over never gets old, and it's always fun to teach and perform!

- ❖ For this trick, you want to start by asking your dog to lie down.

- ❖ Next, take a very high-value treat, get your dog's nose onto the treat, and slowly guide their nose back toward their shoulder, making sure their nose is staying on the treat.

- ❖ As your dog's nose follows the treat back toward their shoulder, they will start to rotate onto one hip.

- ❖ If your dog seems nervous, stop there, give the treat, praise, and repeat!

*  After a couple of repetitions, if your dog is very confident following the treat back and starting to rotate, you're ready to move onto the next step—actually rolling over!

*  Some dogs get nervous at this stage, so go slow with lots of treats and lots of praise. If at any point your dog seems nervous, go back a step to make they are continuing to have fun and remain confident and relaxed.

*  The next step to getting your dog to roll over is to keep their nose on the treat, even letting them lick at the treat, guiding them slowly, gently, and smoothly back toward their shoulder and then over their back. Your dog's head is going to follow the treat, and where the head goes, the body goes.

*  As the treat is lured over your dog's back and they roll over, be sure to click/praise them a lot and give them the treat. As you practice, when your dog's body rotates, you can start to introduce your verbal cue of choice—"roll over," "flip," and "roll" are all great options, but again the verbal cue can be anything of your choosing.

*  As your dog gets more confident, you can begin giving them the verbal cue earlier, as they're down and just starting to roll (as opposed to waiting until they're almost on their back and have already begun the roll).

*  You can also start to phase out your physical cue and lure as your dog becomes more confident and doesn't need to have a treat in their face luring them over. I like to transition into a physical cue of moving my hand in a circle, mirroring on a smaller scale the way we lured our dog when they were first learning.

*  Be careful not to do too many repetitions of this trick in each practice session. Your dog is not only thinking hard, but using muscles they might not normally use. A little goes a long way when practicing this trick!

Tricks to Teach

## Tips

When your dog lies down, if they flop onto one hip, you'll have an easier time teaching them to roll over by going in the direction they are naturally leaning. Most dogs have a side they are more inclined to roll toward. When you're starting, it's best to go in the direction your dog is already leaning/most inclined to turn toward, and later, if you want, you can teach them to roll the other direction.

## Extra Credit

*⁕ Begin to ask your dog to roll over from standing position, instead of first asking them to down position. This is more advanced because your dog is having to chain behaviors together, understanding that they need to change their body's position.

*⁕ You can add this trick into a little skit combining different tricks that your dog knows, like "stop" (stay), "drop" (lie down), and "roll" (roll over), like the classic fire safety message.

*⁕ You can teach your dog to roll in either direction. Most dogs have a side that they are most inclined to roll toward, but there's no reason they can't successfully learn to roll toward the other. You can even put the two directions on different verbal/physical cues, so your dog can tell from your cue which way you want them to roll.

# 32

## Splat

# 32. Splat

This trick is a variation of the classic "play dead" dog trick. I shifted what I teach to splat because I was never comfortable with the original. I like to be thoughtful about what kinds of messages I'm sending with my dog tricks, including being social justice-minded, not using any kind of oppressive homophobic, sexist, or racist stereotypes. I also don't like tricks to be perpetuating anything that encourages violence, so for this trick, I don't use hands in a "gun shape" to cue the trick like many people do, and I don't ask my dog to play dead; instead I ask my dogs to "splat." The goal of this trick is for your dog to lie down and flop onto one side with their face on the ground.

- To start this trick, similar to roll over, you will start with your dog lying down and have yummy tricks ready for luring into the desired position.

- Keep your dog's nose on the cookie and lure their head back over one of their shoulders. Their head will follow their nose and they will start to rotate their whole body.

- As your dog rolls back onto their side, stop rotating your hand and bring it down to the ground. Click/praise and give the treat.

- Your hand position matters a lot for this trick. Be sure you are feeding your dog while in position, meaning you want to praise and give the treat when their body is positioned on their side, and with their head on the ground.

- As you and your dog practice this trick, add in your verbal cue—"splat" and "drop" are a couple of options. Start with using it right as you lure your dog down/over, right before their head touches the ground. The more familiar with the trick your dog gets, you begin verbal cuing earlier and start to fade out the physical luring naturally, as your dog anticipates your lure because they understands the verbal cue.

- Once your dog is familiar with splat, you'll want to start building duration in the trick. We want our dogs to hold the "splat" position until released. Do this by very slowly adding time (second by second) before you click/release your dog to get their treats.

# 33

## Hoop Jump

# 33. Hoop Jump

Chrissy Joy and her dog showing off their hoop jump.

This trick does require an accessory: a hula hoop. You can purchase these at most dollar stores or big-box stores in the spring and summer for just a couple of dollars.

* Show the hoop to your dog and offer treats. You want to make sure that your dog isn't nervous about the hoop. You can also put the hoop on the ground and toss cookies into it to help your dog get more comfortable being around the hoop.

* Stand the hoop up, but keep it on the ground, holding it stable.

- Get your dog's attention and, with your free hand, toss a cookie through the hoop. As your dog goes through, click/praise and let your dog get the treat. Be sure to toss your treats far enough that your dog has to go all the way through—one and a half times the length of your dog is a good length to keep in mind. That amount of space gets your dog all the way through, but not so far that they are likely to get distracted by other things.

- Be sure to practice with your dog going through both sides of the hoop. It looks the same to us, but some dogs get more nervous about going one way than the other. As you practice, keep the hoop on the ground until your dog is very comfortable going through it.

- When your dog is comfortable, start adding in your verbal cue of choice ("hoop," "ring," and "circle" are all common choices). As you introduce the verbal cue, make sure you have your dog's attention, toss the treat, and when you are sure they are committed to going through the hoop, say "hoop." Click and praise as your dog goes through and gets the treat.

- After a few practice sessions, start to ask your dog with the verbal cue and wait to toss the treat until your dog has committed to going through the hoop (instead of before). You want to toss the treat instead of handing it to your dog, so they are looking forward instead of at you. This promotes better and safer jumping.

Veronica Tan's performance dog does an advanced hoop jump.

## Tips

As your dog gets more comfortable with the trick, you can start raising the hoop off the ground, but remember to be careful to not add too much height. See previously mentioned jump height recommendations and safety concerns on page 115.

# 34

## Give Kisses

# 34. Give Kisses

This is a real sweet and feel-good trick. After all, who doesn't love puppy kisses?

*❋ For teaching this trick, you'll want a soft and sticky high-value treat: cream cheese, peanut butter, or something of a similar consistency are great options.

*❋ Start by putting a little bit of the sticky treat onto your hand or your cheek, wherever you would like your dog to lick. It might sound a little gross, but it's worth it!

*❋ Put your hand or cheek in front of your dog, and when they start to lick click/praise and say your verbal cue ("kiss," "lick," "gimme some").

*❋ Repeat several times, using the cream cheese or peanut butter in the location you want the dog to lick.

*❋ When your dog is enthusiastically kissing you with the treats present, give them the verbal cue without the cream cheese or peanut butter. When your dog licks you, click/praise and lots of treats.

# 35
## Spin

# 35. Spin

The end result of this trick is that your dog will spin in circles, going left and right based on your cues. This is a great trick to incorporate into a dance routine with your dog (if you're into that kind of thing) and it's a great one for impressing friends that your dog knows their left from their right!

* Have your dog standing in front of you and put treats in both of your hands that your dog is excited about.

* For this trick you will start by showing your dog the treat, keeping their nose on the treat, and luring them in a wide circle. When they comes back to facing you, click/praise and treat!

* As your dog is following the lure around, you can start adding in your verbal cue (common options include "spin," "turn," "spiral," "round," etc.). I like to teach it just directionally, "left" or "right," so I can use the verbal cue to ask my dogs to spin one way or the other.

* Relatedly, as you are teaching this, you can right away begin introducing spinning in the other direction. Just use the treat in your other hand and lure as described above, adding in a different verbal cue.

* This is a trick that many dogs catch onto quickly, and you will likely be able to start phasing out the lure very quickly and transition it to just the verbal cue and/or a smaller physical cue, like making a small circle with your hand mirroring the larger lure you started with.

* You want to be sure to work left spins and right spins equally. Many dogs tend to naturally favor one direction or the other, so working both is important from the beginning.

## Extra Credit

As your dog gets more comfortable with this trick, you can start to add distance. Start slowly by asking your dog to spin with the verbal and physical cues, praise/click, and treat. Then move back one step and ask them to spin; when they do, click/praise and toss the treat! Move back one step at a time to build distance with the trick. If at any point your dog tries to move toward you before spinning, or gets confused and doesn't spin, just move closer to make sure they can be successful, then add distance again slowly, one step at a time.

# 36
## Shell Game

# 36. Shell Game

Is your dog ready to gamble?! In this trick, your dog is going to be using their nose to find hidden treats and then tell you where the treat is. You will take three containers, put a treat under one, shuffle the containers, and then ask your dog to identify which container has the treat under it.

You will need three identical containers to make sure your dog isn't using the look of a specific container instead of using their nose to find the treat. It will also make the trick look more impressive if you are showing it off to your friends and family. The size and enthusiasm of your dog will determine how sturdy your containers need to be. For small dogs, you can use upside-down paper cups with a hole punched in the top of each. For larger or more exuberant dogs, you will want something more structured, like small plastic flower pots upside down. For whatever containers you select, you will want to have a hole in the bottom to allow the scent of the treat to be more easily identifiable to your dog.

- Start with one container and really smelly treats your dog is excited about. Let your dog watch you put a treat under one container (put the other two containers aside for right now). I like to start with my dog sitting and waiting in front of me.

- Release your dog, and when they sniff at or paw at the container, click/praise and lift the container to let them get the treat. Dogs will often naturally default to a sniff or paw alert. I prefer to reinforce my dogs pawing at the correct container (so wait until they paw to praise/click/treat). However, if you intend to purse competitive scent-work sports, you might want to avoid the pawing, as it can disqualify your dog in a competition.

- Repeat this step several times until your dog is confidently going for the cookie in the container. This is the stage where I also like to introduce a "search" word, so my dog knows I want her to find the treat. Examples of verbal cues include: "search," "find," and "where is it."

* The next step is to introduce a second container, treat under one container, the other one empty. Have your dog settled in front of you in a sit or down and show them both containers, then put a treat under one and release your dog to find it. Do not "shuffle" the containers or move them around yet. If your dog paws/noses (either is completely okay for this trick, different dogs have different search styles) at the right container, lots of praise and immediately lift the container so your dog can get the treat.

* If your dog paws at the empty container, no problem—lift it up and show them there isn't anything there. You don't want to scold your dog—in an upbeat voice, I will usually say something like "whoops, not that one!" (because I talk at my dogs a lot)—then lift the container with the treat and show your dog, but don't let them get to the treat. Sit them again, then release them to search the containers. When your dog selects the right container, lots of praise and lift the container to let your dog get the treat!

* When your dog is consistently alerting to the right container, we want to make things a little more complicated, and make sure your dog is starting to use their nose when identifying what container has the treat, instead of watching you. Settle your dog in front of you, show them that you are putting a treat under one container. Now, while your dog is still waiting in front of you, slide the containers so that, for example, if you started with the container with treats on the right side, after the slide/shuffle, the container with treats will now be on the left side. Release your dog to search for the treats. If your dog alerts on the right container, lots of praise, and immediately lift the container so they can get the treats!

* If your dog alerts to the empty container, again, we don't want to correct them, we just want to show them that the container is empty and the treats were in the other one, but don't allow your dog to get those treats. Reset your dog in front of you and release them to search without re-sliding/shuffling the containers. For some dogs, it takes a few repetitions to understand that not all containers magically produce treats, and that they have to use their noses to figure out which container is going to deliver the payoff!

*• Once your dog is consistently successful in identifying the right container when you are slide/shuffling two containers, you want to add in a third. This is where it starts to look like a much more impressive trick. Start by adding in the third container, but not shuffling/sliding the containers around—just let your dog see you place a treat under one, then release them to search. When they paw or nose bump the correct container, lots of praise and lift the container to let them get the treats.

*• Start changing which container you put treats under without shuffling, so that your dog is having to alert to different container locations and doesn't mistakenly think the game is about alerting to one location. So, for example, the first time, have the treat under the far-right container. The second time, have it under the far-left container, and for the third repetition, have it under the middle container. Vary your rotation so your dog doesn't pick up a pattern!

*• Next, let your dog watch you put a treat under one container, and slide/shuffle the three containers, so that the container with the treat ends up in a different position than when you placed the treat. Release your dog to search, and when they identify the right container, lots of praise and lift the container so they can get the treat. If your dog identifies an empty container, show them it's empty, show them where the right treat is, reset them, and let them search again.

*• Once your dog is consistently identifying the right container, you can get more elaborate in your slides/shuffling of the containers, and your doggo is ready for Vegas!

## Extra Credit

Once your dog is successfully finding the treat hidden under one of three containers, you can begin adding in more containers for them to search for an added challenge.

# 37
## Push

# 37. Push

Ozzie loves to push the ball while playing Treibball.
Photo credit: Thomas Aaron

For this trick you can use any prop you want, but a large exercise ball, a playground ball, or a large beachball are the easiest and can be purchased inexpensively at toy stores or dollar stores, especially in the spring and summer. You want to teach your dog to push the ball with their nose (not bite the ball, pounce on the ball, or paddle the ball with their feet).

* Ask your dog to boop or target your hand with their nose (refer to page 62), reminding them of this trick, especially if it's not one you do often. When your dog nose targets your hand, click/praise and treat.

* Next step is to take the ball in your hands and use the verbal cue you

have for a nose target. Your dog might look a little confused—if they go back to hand targeting, praise and treat, then go back to holding the ball in front of your dog and ask them to nose touch the ball. When your dog touches the ball, click/praise and treat!

* Start to move the ball lower until it is resting on the ground, but still hold it, and ask your dog to nose target. Click/praise and treat them. You can also begin to shift the verbal cue if you want to differentiate it from nose targeting your hand. I like to use "push" for this trick. You could also use something like "soccer" or keep the same verbal nose targeting cue.

* When your dog is consistently nose targeting the ball in your hands, even as the ball is resting on the floor, put the ball in front of them, let go of the ball, and ask them to nose target or push the ball. When your dog's nose touches the ball, click/praise and treat!

* Now that your dog is familiar with the basic concept, you want to start building the strength of their push, because our goal is for your dog's push to be strong enough to move the ball. You might be surprised at how gentle some dogs are with this trick. Even my high-drive Newfoundland, when she was first learning this trick, would touch the ball, but so lightly it wouldn't roll (and this was a giant playground ball). To build strength of push, you want to ask your dog to push the ball a few times and stagger the times when you offer a food reward. Wait to offer treats until they gives a *big* push that moves the ball— then you want to really jackpot your dog, not just with lots of praise (which you should be offering all along), but also lots of treats when they give that big push. By your heavily rewarding the harder they push, your dog will start to offer those pushes exclusively.

## Extra Credit

You can add to this by making it a mini soccer game with your dog. You can get or make a mini soccer net and encourage them to push the ball into the net! This is a great trick to teach if you are thinking about getting involved in the sport of Treibball, which is open to all breeds and mixed breeds and involves "herding" large balls.

# 38

---

# Balance

# 38. Balance

Be sure to only ask your dog to balance soft/safe objects!
Photo credit: Veronica Tan

Want to teach your dog to princess-walk across the room with a book balanced on their head? You can! To start with this trick, though, we will be starting with something light, soft and relatively easy to balance before building up to more complicated objects. Once your dog has mastered the basics of this trick, the sky's the limit for what your dog can balance!

Find an object that you would like your dog to balance. Hacky sacks or floppy plush dog toys work well for this. To start, we want an object that will be easy to keep on your dog's head.

* Get your dog's attention and let them sniff at the object that you are going to put on their head to balance. Make sure it's not something that your dog is going to get stressed or anxious about, especially

when the object is moved toward their head. If your dog is anxious, and in particular if she's anxious about having items moved near or toward their head, like collars or harnesses, you'll want to skip this trick, or move slowly with it, to ensure you aren't causing your dog stress.

* After showing your dog the object you would like them to balance, have it in one hand and a treat they can nibble at in your other hand. Put the nibble treat in front of your dog and let them start to lick/nibble at it, and with your other hand place the object on your dog's head, keeping your hand on the object and verbally praising your dog as the object rests on their head. It may take a little while to find the position where the object will naturally balance. Keep in mind, dogs with longer muzzles/faces will have a different balance point than shorter-nosed dogs like pugs. Only keep the object on your dog for a second, then remove the object and praise/click and treat your dog.

* Begin introducing the verbal cue you want for this trick ("hold," "balance," and "freeze" are all common options for this). At this stage, this verbal cue doesn't hold any meaning for your dog, but begin to add it in while you're holding the treat in front of your dog's nose, right as you place the balance object onto their head, so they associate the balancing behavior with the verbal cue.

* As you work on this trick, you can slowly add duration into the amount of time you ask your dog to balance an object. In the beginning, add time in seconds at a time—don't ask for too much too quickly. This is another trick where less is more. Remember we want to keep our dogs having fun and successful, so starting very slow is going to be the best way to do this.

* As your dog gets more familiar with the trick, you can also begin to move the food lure away briefly. At first, keep the treat on your dog's nose while you place the object you want them to balance, and then give your verbal cue for balance and remove the treat lure. Only pull away for a second praise, return the treat for your dog to nibble/lick at, and remove the balanced object.

Tricks to Teach

*＊ You can also incorporate different objects as you work on this trick, but try to keep the difficulty level of the object you are asking your dog to balance consistent. For example, if your dog is learning to balance a hacky sack, don't suddenly ask them to balance a ruler without slowing down and going back to the early stages, as a ruler will be much more challenging and have a very different center of gravity.

*＊ Over time, as your dog gets more familiar and successful with the trick, you can begin placing the object to balance without the food lure to remind your dog to hold their head straight.

## Safety Note

Be sure not to ask your dog to balance any heavy objects, or objects that are breakable or could otherwise injure your dog if dropped.

This trick is great for helping your dog be comfortable with props—here is Mercury on his fifteenth birthday.

# 39
—
# Carry

# 39. Carry

Do you ever find yourself needing another hand when doing laundry or putting groceries away? Your dog can help! Teaching your dog to carry objects is a useful trick.

* Start with a refresher training session with the "hold trick" taught earlier on page 101. Once your dog is comfortably holding different objects, you can begin asking them to hold the object in different positions. If you have mostly asked your dog to hold things while sitting, see if they can hold while standing.

* If your dog struggles with holding while standing (remember dogs can be very situational in their learning and understanding), go back to the basics with teaching hold, this time working the trick in the new standing position.

* Once your dog is comfortably standing while holding an object and is able to hold with duration (until you ask for the object to be handed to you), we can start adding in movement.

* After asking your dog to hold the object, take a step away from your dog and encourage them to follow you. If the dog drops the object, that's okay, just remind them you want them to hold by handing the object back and quickly ask them to give it to you, praise/click and treat. Then, the next time, again take a step and ask your dog to move forward. When they walk toward you (we're looking for just a step here, not a lot of walking), immediately ask them to hand you the object, click, LOTS of praise and treats! You want to have a little party here because your dog has just combined these tricks together, which is quite tricky!

* Once your dog is consistently able to move one step toward you, try taking multiple steps. You can work this side by side with your dog or with you in front (ideally you will practice both ways so your dog will understand that carrying the object happens no matter where you are in relation to them).

* Start adding difficulty to your training sessions by switching up the objects you ask your dog to carry. Starting with balls and toys, things they are already familiar with having in their mouth, is usually easiest, but you can work up to anything so long as it's not dangerous (please do not ask your dog to carry knives).

* Similarly, the more confident with the trick your dog is, the longer the distances you can ask them to carry objects, and in more distracting environments. Just be sure to reward your dog whenever they carry something for you!

# 40

---

# Learn Object Names

# 40. Learn Object Names

Dogs might not be born knowing how to understand our human languages, but anyone who has ever lived with a dog knows how quickly they can learn to identify words "treat," "dinner," "walk," or "park," to name a few words that many dogs are familiar with. Dogs are experts at studying us and can learn an astonishing number of words. An impressive trick can be for your dog to be able to identify specific toys by name:

- Start to name each of your dog's toys (if your house is anything like mine, that is a lot of toys), and begin using the name of the toy every time they play with it, so for example, "yay ball!" "get the ball" when you throw a tennis ball, or "tug the bunny" if you're playing with a plush bunny, etc. It doesn't matter what you name each toy, but try to be consistent with what you call it so that your dog can start recognizing the names.

- Next, have two toys ready, but start with one your dog plays with a lot. Put it in front of them, and say "get [insert toy name]" so, for example, say "plush bunny." When your dog gets that toy bunny (remember it's the only toy in front of her), click/praise and treat.

- Repeat this a few times; you want your dog to build confidence and have a lot of success getting their plush bunny.

- Now pull out a different toy and put both toys in front of your dog—ask them to get the toy you had been working with, so for our example, put the bunny toy next to a plush doughnut and ask your dog to get the bunny. Because there is a new toy out, your dog might be overstimulated and go to the new toy; that's okay. Don't scold them, just take the toy, pick up the bunny, and play with the bunny with your dog, again verbally reminding them about the bunny's name.

* Next, go back without the doughnut toy, and do a couple of repetitions of getting the bunny with it being the only toy, then add the doughnut back in and ask your dog to get the bunny.

* When your dog gets the bunny, click/praise/treat/have a little party! This is hard stuff!

* When your dog can consistently identify the first toy by name when it is with any other toy, start adding in multiple toys and ask your dog to identify that toy from a grouping of toys (start with three toys, then build up one extra toy at a time). If your dog goes for one of the new toys, back up and do a couple of easy searches with the bunny as the only toy out. When your dog is again successful there, move on to the next level of adding in other toys.

* When your dog has this down, you can begin repeating the process with other toys.

* Eventually your dog will know the names of all their toys and be able to differentiate the bunny from the ball, the doughnut, the lion, the elephant, the lamb, the dinosaur, the dragon, etc. (did I mention my dogs have a lot of toys?).

# 41
—
# Figure Eight

# 41. Figure Eight

For this trick your dog will weave in a figure-eight pattern between your legs. Beware, this trick can be a little tricky if you have an extremely tall dog, and a bit hard on the back to teach if you have a very small dog.

* Start with treats in both of your hands.

* Lure your dog between your legs with one hand keeping your dog's nose on the treat.

* Reach around the back of your leg (turning you a bit into a pretzel) with your other hand, which, remember, also has a treat in it, and lure your dog around to the front.

* When you are comfortable with the luring, start with a couple of treats in each hand and keep your dog moving back around your other leg by luring them through with one hand, and then getting their nose onto the treat in your second hand to finish the figure eight pattern.

* As you're luring, you can start to introduce the verbal cue as your dog is following the treat through and around your legs, and then after a couple of repetitions begin to introduce the verbal cue right before they follow the treat through/around your legs. "Weave," "legs," "between," and "eight" are all common options for cues.

* After a few repetitions, your dog will be familiar with the verbal cue and the behavior you are looking for. At this point you can begin to slowly phase back your luring by pointing to the path between and around your legs that you want your dog to take, instead of needing to bend yourself in a pretzel to lure your dog into position.

# 42

## Leg Weave Walking

# 42. Leg Weave Walking

This trick is an extension of the figure eight trick. It's an impressive one to show off to your friends and a great foundation skill if you ever want to pursue canine freestyle, also commonly referred to as dancing with dogs, which is an internationally popular canine sport. With this trick, your dog is going to be weaving between your legs as you walk. Smaller and more timid dogs may need to go slower when learning this trick as they may be more anxious about accidentally getting stepped on.

* Do a few repetitions of the figure eight trick to remind your dog of the behavior.

* Next, have treats in both hands and send your dog through your legs with your figure eight verbal/physical cue. As they go through your legs and wrap around your first leg, take one step forward with your other leg, so that as they finish the wraparound, they are now going around your leg in front of your body. Treat and praise! For this first repetition, we want just the one step.

* If your dog isn't nervous, repeat, this time taking two steps and using the treats you have in both hands to lure/support your dog as they move through and around your legs.

* When you are first teaching this, you will want to pause/hesitate after each step to make sure your dog has a chance to get through your legs without risk of getting stepped on.

* As your dog gets more familiar with the trick, and more confident that you aren't actually trying to step on them, you can increase the number of steps you are taking between treats. You can also begin to make your steps more fluid, so that your pauses/hesitations phase away and you are able to walk across the room with your dog weaving between your legs.

# 43
—
# Perch Work
# (Circus Elephant Tricks)

# 43. Perch Work (Circus Elephant Tricks)

Although, thankfully, in response to the efforts of animal rights and welfare activists, elephants are no longer used in American circuses, this cute trick gets its name from the circus days of the past. In the finished trick, your dog will pivot around the platform with their front feet on the platform and their rear feet doing the rotation. For this trick you will need a small box or platform that is sturdy enough to support your dog's weight and large enough for your dog to get their front paws up onto. Small plastic one-step step stools from dollar stores work well for this, as do large Tupperware containers (depending on the size/weight of your dog). This trick can be challenging for dogs because, as we have previously discussed, most dogs are front-wheel-drive; where the front feet go, the rear feet follow. With this trick we are asking our dogs to think about their rear feet independently of those front feet. This trick requires rear end coordination and strength.

* Begin by bringing your dog over to the platform and ask them to put "two paws on" (review the paws up trick on page 70).

* Do a couple of repetitions of paws up onto the object and then releasing.

* To begin teaching your dog to pivot, get a treat (for this trick it helps to have very smelly soft treats your dog can nibble at, like cheese or hotdogs) in your hand and, with your dog paws up on the platform, stand facing them. Move the treat slowly to one side; your dog's head should follow it, and where the head goes, so does the body.

* Focus on the placement of your dog's rear feet. For this trick, we want to reward the smallest of steps or movements from those rear feet. Remember this is challenging for your dog, don't try to move too quickly and ask for too much movement too soon.

* When your dog's foot moves, click/praise and treat! Repeat a few times in the same direction, again just looking for one-foot movement before you click/praise and treat.

- Give your dog a break, then ask them to put their front paws back onto the platform, then repeat the above with your dog moving in the other direction. With this trick we want to make sure we work both directions evenly to start with, especially because most dogs will have a direction that they naturally favor, and we want them to understand it's a trick that can be done in both directions.

- Start to introduce your verbal cue for this trick in addition to your luring with the treat on your dog's nose. "Pivot," "slide," and "around" are all good options. Start to introduce that verbal cue right as your dog lifts up their foot.

- With each practice session, slowly build duration, asking for more steps until your dog is able to fully pivot around the platform.

- As your dog gets more familiar with the trick, you can begin to phase out the treat from in front of them and instead ask for the verbal cue. Click/praise and reward as your dog pivots.

## Extra Credit

When your dog is a pro at playing elephant, start adding distance from your dog, so you don't need to be right next to your dog or the platform for your dog to pivot. First start with one step away and reward more frequently than when you were right next to your dog, and build slowly toward being farther away.

# 44

## Push Light

# 44. Push Light

For this trick you'll need a small battery operated "tap light." These are often found in dollar stores, or any hardware store should have them. With this trick, the goal is for you to be able to send your dog to turn the light on and off, either with their nose or with a paw, depending on your preference (and your dog's size). The smallest of dogs will need to use their feet to have enough strength— for example, my chihuahua mix loves this trick, but actually needs to use both of their front feet to turn the tap light on and off, whereas either of my large dogs can do it with one paw or with their nose. I like to teach this trick via the shaping method, where I let my dogs puzzle out with my support what the trick should look like. To do this you will want to have a lot of small but high-value/ smelly treats and either a clicker (clicker training is really helpful for this trick) or your verbal marker ready.

- First, show your dog that the tap light is something that can be turned on and off by pushing it on and off yourself. Then, put the tap light in front of your dog and at first encourage any movement toward/ investigation of the light by clicking and treating.

- By now your dog is used to working with you, and is likely to start offering different behaviors. We want to encourage this by rewarding any kind of engagement with the light with a click/praise and treat.

- When your dog paws or noses hard at the light (depending on your preference for how you want your dog to push it), regardless of whether they push quite hard enough to turn the light on, jackpot! Click, lots of praise, and several treats. Your dog is going to start to quickly figure out that any kind of pressure on the light gets a lot of reward.

- Similarly, when your dog does get the light on for the first time, you want to jackpot that with lots of treats.

- * When your dog is consistently pushing the light on, start to add in your verbal cue. I use "light" for this, but you can use anything you want, like "hit it," "bedtime," etc.

## Extra Credit

When your dog is an expert at turning the light on and off, you can start to add distance, sending your dog from farther away to get the light for you. You can even attach the tap light to your wall and incorporate this trick into the daily comings and goings of your life by asking your dog to get the lights for you.

# 45
---
# Skateboard

# 45. Skateboard

Kelli Whitfield's dogs are ready for the skate park.

Is your hip pooch ready to hit the skate park? Pick up a full-sized or mini skateboard and let's get your dog rolling!

* Start with teaching this trick on carpet or outside on grass, instead of hardwood floors or concrete—this will help your dog keep more control over the skateboard. To start, we want to limit how much the skateboard rolls at first, while your dog is learning the trick and learning to get control over the board, and to keep them from becoming nervous.

*. Ask your dog for that two-paws-up trick up onto the skateboard, praise and treat.

*. Once your dog is familiar and comfortable with the board, move it to a surface where it will be able to roll. Ask your dog to put their front feet on the board. I like to keep one of my feet a few inches in front of the board's front wheels, in case it starts to roll, so it can't go flying and scare my dog. With your dog's front paws on the skateboard, put a treat to their nose and then pull it forward. Our goal is to get one step forward with your dog's feet staying on the skateboard.

*. When your dog moves forward on the board, click/praise and treat!

*. As your dog gets comfortable keeping their feet on the board and moving it forward, they will naturally begin to develop an ability to control the speed and movement of the board. To keep the board moving forward, use a treat in front of your dog and verbally encourage them to come/move toward you.

*. As your dog becomes an expert skateboarder, you can start to phase out the treat in front of your dog. Keep the praise coming and give treats at the end of your ride.

## Safety Note

When you take this trick on the road, you're likely to draw a crowd! Don't forget to continue to obey leash laws. This is for the safety and protection of your dog and the general public. It's not safe for dogs to skateboard while on leash so make sure wherever in public you practice it is safe and legal for your dog to be off leash. Also be sure not to allow your dog to skateboard on busy sidewalks or in the street.

# 46

---

# Cover Your Eyes

# 46. Cover Your Eyes

For this trick we want our dog to take one of their paws, and either paw and swipe, or hold it over one of their eyes. Dogs like Pugs who have very short faces may struggle more with this trick than dogs who have more pronounced muzzles.

- There are a couple of different ways to teach this trick. The way that I grew up learning how to teach this trick was to take a small piece of tape and put it on the dog's nose, right between their eyes.

- When your dog paws at the tape (because it feels funny), you praise/click and treat. As you repeat this, replacing the tape any time it gets knocked off, you start to add in the verbal cue ("eyes," "cover," "shy," whatever you want).

- If you would rather not use tape, or if your dog doesn't notice the little piece of tape on nose and has a strong foundation in targeting, you can also teach without the tape (this is my preferred method). For training with this approach, if your dog knows to paw target to a location that you indicate by pointing, you can touch your dog's muzzle where you want their paw to rest and ask your dog to target. I found this method much faster and easier to use than the tape method with my own dogs.

## Extra Credit

I think this trick is easiest to teach starting with your dog in a "down" position. Next, work on it with your dog when they're sitting, and then when they're standing. These two positions will be a lot more physically challenging for your dog, so you may need to go back to the beginning stages of teaching the trick to keep them from getting confused about what behavior you are looking for.

# 47

# My Dog Can Read

# 47. My Dog Can Read!

Does it sound too good to be true? It's not a trick, you really can teach your dog to read! This is an advanced trick that takes a lot of patience, but it can be done. Sight is not the primary sense that our dogs use to see the world around them; they rely much more on "seeing" the world through their sense of smell, but dogs can actually learn to "read" by identifying simple words.

- Start by creating signs for your dog to read. Pick the names of two or three tricks that your dog knows very well to start with and put each one on a sign. So, for example, maybe "sit," "down," and "wave."

- Have your dog in front of you and have high-value treats ready.

- Show your dog the first sign and, right as you pull out the sign, give the verbal cue for the first trick, for example, "sit." When your dog sits, click/praise and treat!

- Repeat this several times, with your dog getting the verbal cue right as you show the sign.

- Next, pull out the sign without giving your dog the verbal cue. If they sit, click/give lots of praise and lots of treats!

- After your dog has had several days of successful training sessions with this trick, it's time to bring out your second sign. With that sign, let's say "down," proceed the same way you worked with "sit," starting by pairing the sign with a verbal cue, and then phasing out the verbal cue.

- To see if your dog is understanding the difference, once they have been consistently getting the visual written cue without verbal help, after a few days of practice, show your dog the "sit" sign and then, when they're successful (after praise and treats), show them the "down" sign.

- When your dog is consistently accurate between the two signs, do the same thing, adding in the third sign, at first on its own, and then work it in rotation with the other two signs.

## Tip

Pay attention to what your hands and body are doing while you are holding the signs. It can be very easy to inadvertently cue your dog with your hands, or even your eye contact.

# 48
---
# Rebounds

# 48. Rebounds

Haley Deecken's dog Dunkin rocking a rebound off a tree!

Your dog can learn to rebound off walls, trees, etc. For this trick your dog will be using your body as a springboard and do a 180-degree turn (half-turn) off you. This is another physically demanding trick for which you want to consider your dog's overall level of physical fitness and general wellness. This isn't a trick for every dog, and it's a good idea to talk with your veterinarian before pursuing this trick.

- Start with high-value treats, kneeling on the ground. Use your treats to lure your dog onto your knee and then off. To encourage them to move off your knee, you can toss the treat a few inches away. When they bounce off your body, click/praise and either give them the treat or toss it so they can get it.

*⁕* When your dog is consistent, crouch instead of kneeling, slightly increasing the difficulty, and start to add in your verbal cue for the trick ("rebound," "bounce," and "blast" are all options, but again you can call the trick anything you want).

*⁕* When your practice sessions involve your dog consistently rebounding off you while you are crouching, you can stand, but keep your knees bent to give your dog something to aim at. Remember to click/praise and treat and keep your practice sessions short, as this trick is high-impact on your dog's body.

*⁕* As your dog gains confidence in the trick, fade out your physical lure. Just give the verbal cue and/or a small physical cue, and click/praise treat when your dog rebounds!

## Extra Credit

Once your dog is familiar with the trick, you can ask them to springboard off other sturdy objects like walls, trees, or even smaller parts of your body, like your foot! Just make sure the object you are asking your dog to springboard off of is safe, and remember to be respectful in public. Please don't ask your dog to rebound off statues, memorials, gravestones, etc. (I wish I was kidding, but I see videos of people asking their dogs to do this all the time).

# 49

# Chorus Line Kicks

# 49. Chorus Line Kicks

Corinne Andersen's dog is ready to dance!

Is your dog ready for their Broadway debut? Chorus line kicks are a fun interactive trick that is low-impact and very cute. For this trick, your dog will be "kicking" up their front legs to hit your corresponding leg as you kick—essentially their foot targeting your foot.

Tricks to Teach

- To start, have your dog stand facing you.

- Have high-value treats in both of your hands. (This takes a little balance.) Kick one of your feet up, lay your hand on your leg, palm up, and ask your dog to "target" or "high five," depending on which trick they know. When your dog's foot hits your hand or leg, click/praise and treat. Our goal is for your dog to foot target with the foot on the same side as the leg you kick with, so if I kick my right foot, my dog should be foot targeting that leg with their left foot (because they're facing me).

- Next, do the same thing, kicking up your other foot, so your dog is foot targeting your hand/leg with their other foot.

- As you work on repetitions, you can add in your verbal cue (say, "kick," "dance," or "prance") and then start to phase out having your hand on your leg by giving the verbal cue as you kick your leg up with your hands at your side. When your dog "kicks" your leg, click/praise and treat!

## Extra Credit

The more familiar with the trick your dog is, the faster you can go, and you can begin to build endurance with the kicks, say, by asking your dog to do a couple of kicks before you treat. Once your dog is responding confidently to the verbal cue, you can also transition to your dog to chorus-kicking at your side and just kicking air, instead of facing you and kicking your legs.

# 50
—
# Drawing

# 50. Drawing

Last Christmas, when I was visiting with my moms, they commented that I had never given them grandchildren. I commented that I had, reminding them of

my three dogs. "But they can't color and do crafts with me," (like other children in their lives do) they said. I then reminded them that actually my dogs can color with them, and...there was no response to that but to agree that I was right. My dogs love their grandmas and are always happy to color pictures for them. There's nothing like having art on your wall that was painted by your dogs! You can do this trick with paints, but I like to do it with washable markers because it's much less messy and easier to manage in a small space.

When teaching this trick to your dog, it's easiest if you make a "handle" for your paintbrush or markers, creating a "T" shape with the marker sticking forward and a horizontal crossbar that your dog can hold in their mouth. This can be made in a variety of ways, by attaching a wooden dowel with duct tape, or the easiest way I've found is to take an empty toilet paper or paper towel cardboard tube, punching a hole through one side of it with a pencil, and pushing the back end of the marker into the hole, leaving the marker tip end sticking out. This method also makes it easy to switch out markers so your dog can draw in different colors without you having to create multiple handles.

- Start by asking your dog to hold the marker attachment, then to give it to you. Praise/click and treat.

- Next, ask your dog to nose target the paper. I find that, for this, using a watercolor paper book that's hard, or taping the edges of a piece of plain white paper to a binder or clipboard, helps to give structure. Praise/click and treat when your dog's nose touches the page.

- Now ask your dog to hold the marker again, and cue them to target the paper. The minute the marker touches the page, praise/click and treat! Your dog is ready to draw!

- You can start to add in a new verbal marker for this trick, like "draw," "paint," or "create," and don't forget to change out the marker to different colored ones to create paintings that match your decorating style.

- Rotate the canvas as your dog paints, and/or point to specific areas of the paper you want your dog to target the marker or paintbrush to.

Charlotte the modern artist with her drawing.

## Extra Credit

These drawings make great gifts for friends and family. Your dog could even have their own gallery showing to raise money for a favorite charity, rescue, shelter, or dog-focused program.

# Chapter 5

# Taking Tricks to the Next Level

In the past year, the sport of trick training has been getting international attention, thanks in large part to the success of celebrity dog trainer Sara Carson and her dog Hero's successful performances on the TV show *America's Got Talent*. Sara has taken trick training to the next level, showcasing the amazing skills of her dogs and bringing their lively, impressive performances into millions of living rooms across the country and around the world. Sara is one of the most sought-after dog trainers in the world and was kind enough to sit down with me to discuss her experience with trick training and what it was like to do tricks with her dogs on stage at *America's Got Talent*:

Sara Carson and her Super Collies.

SASSAFRAS. How did you get involved in trick training?

SARA. I started to watch dog trick and agility videos on YouTube. I got hooked and enjoyed teaching my family dog.

SASSAFRAS. How have dog tricks changed the life of you and your dogs?

SARA. It has helped build a stronger bond and created a better form of communication for me and my dogs.

SASSAFRAS. What kinds of places have you and your dogs performed?

SARA. We have performed at casinos, half-time shows, theme parks and theaters!

SASSAFRAS. What was it like to be on *America's Got Talent* with your dogs?

SARA. It was a lot of work, but a very fun experience. We met several new friends, and the dogs had a great time! It was a much larger scale than we are used to, so that was a fun training opportunity.

SASSAFRAS. What are your dogs' favorite tricks?

SARA. All of my dogs love to jump! Any trick that involves them getting some air is definitely their favorite!

SASSAFRAS. What is your favorite trick to teach?

SARA. I love teaching a walking handstand. It takes a lot of time and patience to help build up the dog's muscle memory and to get them to understand what is being asked.

SASSAFRAS. What advice would you like to give to someone just starting to train tricks?

SARA. Just have fun—stop saying so much and trying to give your dog information that they don't understand. Patience is key, and be sure to reward any efforts that the dog offers.

# Tricks as Sports

Tricks are something that anyone can do with dogs. As you and your dogs have already discovered, they are a great way for you to have fun together. Tricks are also one of the fastest-growing dog sports. There are now multiple organizations where you and your dogs can compete in the sport of tricks, earning titles (and colorful ribbons and prizes)! As someone with a background in dog training, I had a lot of fun training and competing in canine sports, so trick titles were a natural progression for me. I'm not what I would consider a particularly competitive person, but I like having training goals, and I found that trick titles were a great way to structure my training goals with my dogs.

Think you might want to compete with your dog? Here's how to get started! There are currently two main organizations that sanction trick title competitions.

## Do More with Your Dog (DMWYD)

This is the oldest and largest trick dog title organization and, in many ways, can and should be credited with the explosion of trick training we are seeing across the world. Trick titles from DMWYD can be earned via video or in person after being approved by a Certified Trick Dog Instructor (CTDI). The levels of trick titles currently available are: Novice, Intermediate, Advanced, Expert, and Champion. DMYWD trick titling is open to all dogs regardless of age or breed, and mixed breeds are

Sirius is only the second Newfoundland in the world to earn her Trick Dog Champion Title (TDCH).

encouraged to compete, as dogs with disabilities are encouraged to be involved in the sport. Each level of trick title has a specific number of tricks and kinds of tricks that must be performed for the title to be issued.

The ability to earn trick titles via video was what initially drew me to get involved with DMWYD because it was so accessible. My dog Charlotte excels at trick training but, because of her traumatic start in life as a street dog, is extremely dog-reactive and highly stressed around unfamiliar dogs. Needless to say, I wouldn't ever ask her to go to a dog show. DMWYD trick titles have been an amazing way for Charlotte to thrive in this growing sport, and for us to have a lot of fun together along the way. The supportive nature of the community of trainers and competitors is what encouraged me to become more and more involved, eventually becoming a Certified Trick Dog Instructor myself to support other people exploring the sport, beginning in 2013.

Do More with Your Dog worked with the American Kennel Club to develop their Trick Dog titling program, so DMWYD trick titles are grandfathered into the AKC trick titling levels. Meaning that if you earn DMWYD titles, you can transfer those titles over to AKC (Novice through Trick Dog Performer level). The DMWYD Trick Dog Champion title is earned via video that is submitted directly to DMWYD to be reviewed by staff. All information about Do More with Your Dog titles can be found on their website, www.DoMoreWithYourDog.com.

## American Kennel Club

In 2017, the American Kennel Club (AKC) began offering their own trick dog titling program. The AKC is the world's largest and oldest not-for-profit all-breed registry, and what many people think of when "dog shows" come to mind. Contrary to popular assumptions, mixed-breed dogs can and do participate in AKC performance sport events, including trick titles. AKC trick titles at the lower levels (novice, intermediate, advanced, and trick dog performer) must be witnessed in person by a CGC (Canine Good Citizen) evaluator. The trick dog elite performer title must be filmed and submitted to AKC staff for review and approval for that title to be issued.

To learn more about AKC Trick Dog Titles, visit www.akc.org/sports/trick-dog.

# Tricks That Can Translate to Sports

Trick dog training is a sport in its own right, but it can also be a fantastic gateway opportunity for you and your dog to get involved with other sports together. There are an ever-growing number of canine sports with training opportunities and trial or show opportunities in cities around the country. To start getting involved, look for training classes taught by trainers in your area that use positive-reinforcement training methods only. Avoid "balanced" trainers who use aversive methods, or anyone who suggests use of prong collars, e-collars, or punishment. Trick training is about building a stronger relationship between you and your dog. There are a variety of sports that you and your dog might be interested in that utilize some of the same skills as trick dog training. These sports include:

## Obedience
Competitive obedience is a sport where dog and handler teams follow specific routines such as heeling, stays, etc. Obedience is a precision sport showcasing the ability of a dog and handler team to work together.

My dog Sirius loves rally obedience.

## Rally

Rally is an obedience-based sport that features some traditional obedience, but is more playful. Rally obedience involves a new routine combining obedience skills with a twist that is very reminiscent of trick training.

## Musical Freestyle

Also frequently called dancing with dogs, musical freestyle involves incorporating trick behaviors into routines set to music where dogs and handlers are "dancing" together.

## Rally Freestyle Elements

A fairly young sport that combines many of the trick behaviors that are used in the sport of Canine Musical Freestyle with a structured course set by the judge that resembles Rally Obedience.

Dog agility is a fast-paced athletic sport.
Photo credit: Barb Wright

## Agility

One of the most popular and well-known canine sports. In dog agility, dogs race over, around, and through a rainbow of obstacles as directed by the running handler. Trick training can be a great foundation for getting started in agility, especially in terms of engaging with found obstacles and increasing a dog's confidence, which translates well to agility.

Treibball is a fun sport where dogs like Ozzie channel their herding instincts by herding balls.

Photo credit: Thomas Aaron

## Treibball

It's like herding without sheep! In Treibball, any breed (or mix) can participate, even if they wouldn't normally be considered a herding dog. In this sport, dogs are trained to "herd" and move large balls around a field and into a goal. Treibball is a lot of fun for dogs of all sizes, and builds on some of the tricks we learned in this book, like "push" (page 151).

Leia practicing parkour skills.
Photo credit: Lenore Pawlowski

## Parkour

One of the newest dog sports, parkour has many roots and commonalities with trick training mixed with agility. Trick training is an excellent foundation for the sport, where your dog can earn titles by engaging physically with different environmental features like logs, rocks, park benches, etc.

Charlotte loves to learn skills that involve using her nose.

## Nose Work/ Scent Work

Our dogs really "see" the world through their noses. Dogs' noses are incredibly powerful. Dogs are capable of finding missing people, finding bed bugs, and detecting cancer (yes, really!), as well as sniffing out narcotics and explosives. In addition to these real-world jobs that dogs and their noses do, there are also recreational sports like tracking and nose work/scent work that channel your dog's natural scent abilities! These sports are great for all dogs, regardless of age or physical ability. The shell-game trick we learned is a great introduction for your dog to the fun and growing sport of nosework.

It can be overwhelming to think about getting involved with these sports, but it can be a lot of fun, and training programs and trails (that's generally what performance dog shows are called) are available near or in most every community. You can learn more about dog sports by visiting the American Kennel Club's website and checking other national organizations to find out about local clubs and organizations in your area. You can also go to any dog show (without your dog). Shows are a great way to see these sports in action, meet competitors in your local area, find out where they train, and learn more about how to get involved with your own dog.

## Performing/Therapy Dogs

Trick dogs bring joy to everyone watching them, whether it's your friends and family in the comfort of your home, or charming millions of viewers on TV. If you and your trick dog are interested in taking your show on the road, there are a variety of opportunities for you to shine in the spotlight together. Local, regional, and national talent shows are a great way to show off your dog's trick routines. If you and your dog want to use your tricks to support people in need, you can also begin the process of finding out if your dog has the right temperament to train toward being a therapy dog.

Therapy dogs visit, comfort, and entertain people in hospitals, assisted living facilities, schools, and a variety of other places. Becoming a certified therapy dog team usually involves some structured training classes to make sure that your dog is going to be a good fit for this kind of work, which can be very high-stress. Your dog will need to be very comfortable being approached and handled by a variety of strangers, and remain calm in a variety of settings like hospitals and around other dogs and people of all ages. Therapy Dogs International (www.tdi-dog.org) is a great organization that can connect you with resources in your local community to get started.

## Movie Stars

Animal actors appearing in our favorite TV shows and movies are actually some of the greatest trick dogs! Animal actors are trained to perform various behaviors (a.k.a. tricks) cued by their handlers out of sight of the camera. Animal actors have to not only be skilled trick performers, but also be able to handle doing those tricks in a variety of settings and around all kinds of equipment, and not be stressed out about being in new situations.

Think your dog has what it takes to be a star? There are talent agencies that represent talented dogs across the country and are always looking for canine actors for print, TV, film, and stage roles.

To learn more about the life of a trick dog actor, I spoke with one of my training mentors, Frankie Joiris, whose dogs regularly appear on television, to learn more about what it takes for trick dogs to become actors.

Frankie Joiris and her dog Lingo.

SASSAFRAS. How long have you been training dogs?

FRANKIE. Professionally for forty-two years, but I started training them about four years before that.

SASSAFRAS. How long have you been training animal actors?

FRANKIE. Forty years.

SASSAFRAS. What sorts of gigs have your trick dogs had (stage, screen, commercials, etc.)?

FRANKIE. I can't even begin to answer that, we've done all of the above as well as art installations, nightclubs, etc.

SASSAFRAS. If someone wanted to get into animal acting with their trick dog, what advice would you give them?

FRANKIE. Contact theatrical animal agents in your area and see if you can shadow them on a few shoots to see if this is something you really want to do.

SASSAFRAS. How did you get started with trick dog training?

FRANKIE. It was a natural offshoot of the other types of training I do.

SASSAFRAS. How do you incorporate tricks into the acting work your dogs do?

FRANKIE. Teaching tricks is a great way to keep the dog motivated to learn new things all the time.

SASSAFRAS. What sorts of places have your dogs performed?

FRANKIE. Nightclubs, theaters, universities, dog events, parties, art galleries.

SASSAFRAS. What is it like for dogs to do tricks on set?

FRANKIE. Often the dog is required to make slight changes in their behavior for each shot, so it's important that the dog love the process of learning and repeating while paying attention to the handler, and that the dog does not think it's cute to toss out random tricks just because you've got a treat handy. No one on set will think it's cute if your dog rolls over when he was supposed to play dead.

SASSAFRAS. What are your dog's favorite tricks?

FRANKIE. Most of my dogs love the difficult tricks most, because they put in such effort to learn them.

SASSAFRAS. What is your favorite trick to teach dogs?

FRANKIE. Whichever trick is going to challenge that individual dog's mind the most, so it really depends on which dog. Things that require the dog to be thoughtful. I can't stand tricks that encourage dog to throw random behaviors hoping to be right.

Sassafras. What advice would you give to someone just starting to train tricks?

Frankie. Believe in yourself. With the right guidance, there's nothing you can't do with your dog.

Sassafras. Anything else you would want readers to know about trick dog training?

Frankie. Use trick training to better understand your dog and your relationship, there is so much to learn!

Even if your dog doesn't have what it takes to be on the silver screen, or you aren't interested in being a stage parent, thanks to the advent of social media and the ease with which we can record and share our trick dogs' successes (and bloopers) with our friends, and with the world, trick dogs are extremely popular on Instagram and YouTube. So don't be afraid to show off your dog's tricky skills to new and old friends online!

## Let's Get Tricky!

Regardless of what your goals in training your dog may be—to find a fun way to spend time with your dog, impress your friends, collect a bunch of ribbons or become a performer—tricks are something every dog can do. I hope that in these pages you have found new ways to communicate more clearly with your dog(s), had a lot of fun along the way, and gotten ideas for how you can (should you choose to do so) translate these tricks into involvement with other dog sports. As you and your dog know by now, dog trick training is for every person and every dog. It's fun for the whole family, or a great way to spend a quiet evening at home with your best friend. It is my sincere hope that the tricks you've learned here will only be the beginning of a new and deeper relationship between you and your dog.

# Acknowledgements

The sky's the limit with trick training!
Photo credit: Kathleen Tepperies

First and foremost, I want to thank the amazing trick dog trainers from around the world who shared beautiful photographs of their dogs for inclusion in this book. Your photographs have brought the joy of tricks to life on the page, and I'm so grateful that you have shared your dogs with all of us.

On a personal level, I want to thank the dogs who have built and shaped my life from my earliest memories. These include the dogs that I have shared my life with in the past—Peepers, Snickers, Flash, Sydney, and Cosmo—and the dogs who currently bring joy to my daily life: Mercury (my retired service dog), Charlotte TDCH, Parkour L1, and Sirius TDCH, CGC, TKP. I also want to thank the celebrity trick dogs who have inspired me, especially Lassie: Pal, the first dog to play Lassie, and his (yes, Lassie has always been played by a male dog) direct descendants Lassie Junior, Spook, and Baby, who starred in the show during the 1950s and 1960s and whose character, via television reruns, was my childhood hero, along with his trainer, Rudd Weatherwax.

I'd like to give a special thank-you to my dog trainer beta readers, Milo Jordan, Kelli Whitfield, and Saranique Schwartz. Thank you to all of the dog trainers who have supported me and my passions since I was a junior handler. A special thank you to my patrons and also to Frankie Joiris, one of my trainers and mentors from when I lived in NYC, and her dog, my god-dog-ter, Kiss-Me. I also want to thank all of the rescues and breeders who have entrusted me with the amazing dogs who have changed my life.

Last and certainly not least, thank you to my partner Kestryl, who is not only the best doggie co-parent I could ever dream of, but who also has always supported all of my dog-related dreams, including giving up weekend mornings to sit at training classes and dog shows and supporting our family so I could commit to writing (often about dogs) full-time.

# About the Author

Sassafras and her dogs: Mercury (Sassafras' retired Service Dog), Charlotte TDCH, L1 Parkour, and Numa's Sirius Whimsy TDCH, CGC, TKP

Sassafras Lowrey is a celebrated author and Certified Trick Dog Instructor. Sassafras has been involved with training dogs for twenty years and has trained and competed in a variety of canine sports, including Dog Agility and Rally Obedience as well as Canine Parkour and Tricks.

Sassafras has written regularly for an array of local and national dog and pet lifestyle magazines, including *The Bark*, *Dogster* and *Whole Dog Journal*. Sassafras and her dogs spent many years living in New York City and now live, write, and train in Portland, Oregon.

Learn more at: www.SassafrasLowrey.com.

Printed in the USA
CPSIA information can be obtained
at www.ICGtesting.com
JSHW012010140824
68134JS00023B/2355